The Vegetarian Bible

Publications International, Ltd.

Recipe development on pages 82, 110, 200 and 230 by Carissa Kinyon.

Recipe development on pages 80, 100, 170 and 240 by Marilyn Pocius.

Photography on pages 39, 41, 61, 81, 83, 89, 95, 101, 111, 121, 127, 151, 157, 171, 173, 179, 201, 205, 223, 227, 231, 235, 237, 241 and 247 by PIL Photo Studio.
Photographer: Tate Hunt
Photographer's Assistant: Justin Paris
Food Stylists: Dianne Freeze, Carol Smoler
Assistant Food Stylists: Michael Deuson, Sheila Granne, Breana Moeller

Ingredient, equipment and portrait photography on pages 4–27 by Christopher Hiltz.

Pictured on the front cover *(top to bottom):* Portobello & Fontina Sandwiches *(page 216)* and Thai Seitan Stir-Fry *(page 86).*
Pictured on the back cover *(counterclockwise from top):* Vegetarian Summer Rolls *(page 84),* French Carrot Quiche *(page 240)* and Black Beans & Rice-Stuffed Poblano Peppers *(page 150).*

Contributing writer: Marilyn Pocius

Cover and title page illustration by Shutterstock.
Photography on page 5 by Thinkstock, LLC.
Photograph of cutting board on page 16 ©1998 PhotoSpin.

ISBN-13: 978-1-4508-7557-8
ISBN-10: 1-4508-7557-2

Library of Congress Control Number: 2013937073

Manufactured in China.

8 7 6 5 4 3 2 1

Microwave Cooking: Microwave ovens vary in wattage. Use the cooking times as guidelines and check for doneness before adding more time.

Preparation/Cooking Times: Preparation times are based on the approximate amount of time required to assemble the recipe before cooking, baking, chilling or serving. These times include preparation steps such as measuring, chopping and mixing. The fact that some preparations and cooking can be done simultaneously is taken into account. Preparation of optional ingredients and serving suggestions is not included.

pil
Publications International, Ltd.

Table of Contents

What Does it Mean to Be Vegetarian?

Vegetarian, at least as defined for this book, means consuming no meat, poultry or fish. But there are many kinds of vegetarians and hundreds of reasons for being one. A recent study estimates that about 3.2 percent of adults in the U.S. (7.3 million people) follow a vegetarian-based diet; 15 million more say they follow a vegetarian-inclined diet. More people, especially young ones, are embracing a vegetarian lifestyle every day.

About half of the surveyed vegetarians said that the main reason they eat a plant-based diet is to improve overall health. A diet filled with veggies, fruits, grains and nuts tends to be lower in saturated fat than a meat-based diet and higher in fiber and antioxidants as well. We all know we should be eating more vegetables—it's the advice given by every nutritionist and on every food pyramid. Becoming vegetarian, even if it's only part time, is a great opportunity to do just that.

Sure there are health and environmental benefits to giving up meat, but one of the unsung joys of cooking vegetarian dishes is the incredible flavors you'll discover. There is so much variety in terms of color, taste and texture in the plant kingdom. When a meal isn't centered around meat, it's easier to appreciate the sweet tenderness of a roasted beet or the crunch of just-picked sugar snap peas. It's astonishing how delicious vegetables can be when prepared with recipes designed to make the most of them. Meat eaters don't know what they're missing when they dismiss vegetables as boring side dishes. There's nothing boring about Spinach Soufflé (page 80) or Cheese Ravioli with Wild Mushroom Sauce (page 120)!

Why Did You Become a Vegetarian?

"I became a vegetarian at 12 after reading *Charlotte's Web.*" —Colleen Briedrick

Religion and Vegetarianism

India has the world's largest population of vegetarians. This is no surprise since it is the birthplace of Hinduism, Jainism and Buddhism. All three of these religions favor vegetarianism as part of their nonviolent philosophy. Hare Krishnas, Seventh Day Adventists and Quakers also promote a plant-based diet.

Spinach Soufflé, pg. 80

The Many Flavors of Vegetarianism

Mainstream vegetarians are sometimes referred to as lacto-ovo vegetarians. (Lacto stands for milk; ovo for eggs.) They eat eggs, milk and dairy products in addition to plant-based foods. Lacto-vegetarians consume milk products, but not eggs. Pescatarians consume fish and other seafood, in addition to dairy and eggs. Vegans eat only plant-based foods—no dairy, eggs, cheese or honey. See page 8 for more information on the vegan diet.

Flexitarians are semi-vegetarians. They eat meat occasionally in small amounts, but derive the bulk of their calories from plants. This is a group that is growing in numbers rapidly as more people omit meat from their daily meals for health or environmental reasons.

Health is the most common reason for going vegetarian, but concern for animals is also part of the motivation. Many animal rights supporters simply feel that it is morally indefensible to kill animals for food. For others, the very idea of meat becomes repulsive once they accept reality—the shrink-wrapped pork chops in the meat case came from a cute pink pig, like Babe or Porky. In the age of instant information we can't ignore where our food comes from; the more we know about factory farms, mad-cow disease, E. coli contamination and the like, the more we lose our appetite for steak.

Vegetarian Goes Mainstream

Gone are the days when a vegetarian had to visit a strange smelling, brightly lit health food store to buy provisions. Now any decent size market stocks soymilk, quinoa, veggie burgers and even seitan. Certainly there are more vegetarians than ever, but there are also a lot of people who want the benefits of a vegetarian diet but don't want to commit to it 100 percent. As they discover how delicious vegetarian cuisine can

be, they want to have their tofu and eat chicken, too. Some people simply give up beef and pork (these folks are sometimes labeled "pollotarians"). Others are vegetarian most of the time but break the rules for special occasions or when a serious craving hits.

Whether they're called flexitarians or semi-vegetarians, these advocates of eating less meat are a huge segment of the population. Often they transition to becoming true vegetarians. Almost always they realize that vegetarian cuisine can open up whole new worlds of flavor and enjoyment.

Diet for a Small Planet

American vegetarianism really caught on in 1971 with the publication of a runaway bestseller by Frances Moore Lappé—*Diet for a Small Planet.* The book encouraged people to give up meat because it wasted resources that could be used to feed a hungry world. It inspired millions. Vegetarian cookbooks, restaurants, co-ops and communes became commonplace.

Planning Vegetarian Meals

For some time now, American meals have consisted of a main course—meat—accompanied by sides. The newly minted vegetarian may, at first, simply replace the center-of-the-plate meat with a veggie lasagna or tofu dog. A meal certainly doesn't have to be structured that way. It doesn't even have to be served on one big plate! In fact, most cuisines around the world are considerably less meat-centric. In Chinese and Japanese cooking, meat is more often considered a condiment or flavoring agent than the star of the show. The Middle East has its small plates called mezes and Spain specializes in tapas.

Vegetarian meals work well as a series of individual dishes that complement each other without a single item stealing the show. Soup, salad and a crusty loaf of bread can be a filling and delightful dinner. A vegetable gratin, a colorful stir-fry or a cheese soufflé could be the centerpiece for an elegant dinner party. The possibilities are endless.

"When I ate meat I used to ask my mom what kind of animal it came from. Her answer was always, 'I prefer to think that it grows on trees.' I was too aware of what it really was and I knew I couldn't do it anymore."
—Christa Baker

Color it Delicious

There are more colorful options to choose with veggies, fruits and grains than you would ever find with meat. Variety is an important ingredient in any meal, especially a vegetarian one. Choosing a colorful array of foods doesn't just look pretty, it provides a good range of vitamins, minerals and micronutrients. The colors can come in a series of smaller dishes—a green salad, cornbread, black beans and rice—or you can mix colorful vegetables in an Asian-style stir-fry or other main course.

Think Different

Think out of the box when it comes to traditional dishes. A salad doesn't have to be the standard lettuce with dressing. It can also be an exotic Quinoa & Mango Salad (page 198), sliced tomatoes with avocado or just an assortment of crisp raw veggies. Turn a favorite vegetable into a casserole or gratin to make it more filling. Resize an appetizer recipe and call it a main course (or vice versa). If you've got a taste for a popular meat-containing dish like lasagna or fajitas, indulge in it vegetarian style. Try Skillet Vegetable Lasagna (page 130) or Seitan Fajitas (page 174).

Seitan Fajitas, pg. 174

The Vegetarian Pantry

All cooking depends on the quality of ingredients—even more so if it's vegetarian. The sometimes subtle flavors of fresh produce need to be coaxed and complemented, not overwhelmed. Use cheap oil or a dusty jar of dried basil and it will be easy to tell. The flavor of meat can mask a multitude of sins!

For the recipes in this book, here are some pantry items you should keep on hand:

 **Asian noodles:** rice noodles, soba

 Beans: a variety of canned or dried

 Bulgur wheat

 Chickpeas

 Cornmeal

 **Dried mushrooms**

 Lentils

 Oils: extra virgin olive oil vegetable oil

 Pasta

 Quinoa

 Rice: long grain, brown, basmati, jasmine

 Soy sauce

 Tomatoes: canned whole and diced

 Vegetable broth

Vegan Cooking

In addition to eliminating meat, fish and poultry from their diets, vegans also cut out other animal products, including dairy, eggs and honey. Dairy products are usually the most difficult to replace. For most recipes, soymilk or other dairy-free milk can be substituted one for one. Butter can often be replaced with dairy-free margarine, but read labels carefully since many margarines contain milk products in the form of casein or whey. There are vegan forms of mayonnaise readily available.

Cheese is trickier. It can usually be left out entirely if it's only a topping or minor part of the recipe. Cheese alternatives are available but don't always taste or melt like cheese and texture can be a problem if they are an important element in the recipe. For gratins or casseroles, try a bread crumb or nut topping in place of cheese. Crumbled tofu is also a possibility. See the recipe for Greek Salad with Dairy-Free "Feta" (page 202) for one method of flavoring tofu to stand in for cheese.

Commercial vegan egg replacements are available. (Don't be fooled by the cholesterol-free egg substitutes in the dairy case; they're egg whites.) Many recipes, including soufflés and fritattas, can't be recreated without eggs. For others, especially baked goods than use no more than 3 eggs, fruit purées or silken tofu are good substitutes. Use ¼ cup of tofu, ¼ cup of applesauce or one mashed banana to fill in for one egg.

 Many recipes in this book are naturally vegan. They are marked with a special icon. Many other recipes can be made vegan fairy easily and for those a variation is given.

Vitamins and Minerals

Every diet needs variety to be healthy. A vegetarian diet consisting of macaroni and cheese and pizza would certainly not provide the vitamins, minerals and other nutrients human bodies need. A diet of fast food burgers, fried chicken and soda would be even worse! See the chart on page 11 for some sources of nutrients most often derived from animal products that are of particular concern to vegetarians. Vegans have to be even more aware. Vitamin B-12 especially can be hard to obtain for those who omit dairy and eggs.

The key to healthy eating is the same for vegetarians, vegans, flexitarians and meat eaters: enjoy a wide variety of food every day.

Vegan Pesto, pg. 110

Gazpacho, pg. 36

Socca, pg. 74

What about Wine?

Enjoying a glass of wine with dinner is certainly a pleasure that shouldn't be denied vegetarians. The rules for pairing are in the same spirit as for a meat-based meal, but instead of red with meat, white with poultry and fish, serve heavier red wines with hearty, starchy dishes and whites with lighter green vegetable dishes. As always, your own preferences are the only important deciding factor.

These wines pair well with...	these dishes
crisp clean whites (Sauvingon Blanc, Champagne, Pino Grigio)	veggie risottos, quiches, pasta primavera
full-bodied whites (Chardonnay, Viognier)	creamy, rich dishes, fettucine Alfredo
fruity reds (Beaujoulais, Merlot, Rioja)	bean and cheese dishes, mushroom dishes
hearty reds (Chianti, Cabernet, Zinfandel)	lasagna, root vegetables, chillies and hearty soups, lentils

"It just hits you: we don't need animal products. Vegetarians are healthier, and our diets positively impact the environment as well."

—Jenny Inzerillo

Keep Things Interesting

1. Serve three or four small plates instead of one main course plus sides.

2. Go ethnic. Explore vegetarian Italian pastas and risotto, Asian stir-fries, Mexican bean dishes or French soufflés.

3. Serve breakfast for dinner. Eggs, waffles and pancakes taste great late.

4. Give potatoes and pasta a rest. Try adding couscous, quinoa, barley, bulgur wheat and brown rice to your repertoire.

5. Experiment with meat replacements, including tofu, seitan and tempeh.

6. Cook with the seasons. Take advantage of farmers' markets and enjoy fresh produce every day.

The Healthy Vegetarian Diet

Vegetarianism has come a long way from the dark days when it was considered a sort of fringe behavior that often involved living in a commune. Even fast food spots now offer vegetarian options. In fact, the American Dietetic Association, a fairly conservative organization, recently issued a position paper that said appropriately planned vegetarian diets are "healthful, nutritionally adequate, and may provide health benefits in the prevention and treatment of certain diseases." The paper added that being vegetarian was appropriate for just about anyone, including children, adolescents, pregnant women and athletes.

"When I was 30, I felt that I had too many ailments and was slightly overweight. By becoming a vegetarian, I solved the problem of my weight, ailments and also 95 percent of my allergies."
—Keith Browne

The Protein Problem that Isn't

Some of the old myths never die, and if you've been a vegetarian for any length of time you've probably been asked, "But what do you do about protein?" Our meat-centric society generally thinks of beef, pork and chicken as the only "good" sources of protein.

Protein is part of the structure of every cell in our bodies. When protein from food is digested it is broken down into amino acids. These in turn are reassembled into the proteins our body uses. Decades ago it was believed that since meat contained all the essential amino acids (see the sidebar for a definition), vegetarians needed to eat a combination of foods at each meal that provided this same assortment. *Diet for a Small Planet* and other books of the time called this "protein combining." It was complicated and soon found to be unnecessary.

"If I've proved anything by not eating meat for the past 20 years, it's that nothing needs to die to keep me alive."
—Tom Appel

While plant sources don't contain all 10 amino acids, they do contain an assortment. As long as you eat a variety of food every day and get enough calories, your metabolism will take care of the combining for you. There's no reason for vegetarians who are eating a wholesome diet to worry about protein intake. In fact, next time someone asks you about it, you might point out that most Americans get too much protein, which can definitely be unhealthy.

What's an essential amino acid?

The human body can produce the amino acids it requires to make protein, except for eight of them. These are called the essential amino acids and must be obtained from food. Animal products contain all eight. Most plant sources lack some of them. The exceptions are soybeans and quinoa, which, like meat, are complete proteins.

Know Your Nutrients

Here's a list of good sources of nutrients sometimes missing from a vegetarian diet.

Protein	Vitamin B-12	Zinc
dairy products	dairy products	legumes
eggs	eggs	nuts
legumes	enriched soymilk	soy products
lentils	fortified cereals	sprouts
soy products	nutritional yeast	whole grains
whole grains		wheat germ

Calcium	Iron*
broccoli	beans, peas and lentils
dairy products	dried fruit
enriched soymilk	enriched cereals
kale	kale
spinach	spinach
	whole grains

To enhance iron absorption, combine these foods with those rich in Vitamin C.

What's Nutritional Yeast?

It's not for making bread rise! Nutritional yeast is a favorite with vegetarians, especially vegans, since it has a taste similar to Parmesan cheese and can be a source of vitamin B-12. It comes in powder or flake form and can be sprinkled directly on food or used in recipes. Read labels carefully though, since only a few brands are fortified with B-12. The tongue twister of the chemical name for B-12 you should look for is cyanocobalamin.

Vegetable Basics

Fresh vs. Frozen vs. Canned

Say yes to all three! Fresh produce picked at the peak of ripeness is certainly the tastiest and most nutritious choice. Too bad we don't all have year-round vegetable gardens in our backyards. In the real world there are plenty of times when fresh just isn't an option. Frozen vegetables are usually picked at peak ripeness and blanched before flash freezing so they retain most of their vitamins and minerals. In fact, frozen can be better for you than out of season produce that's traveled cross-country losing nutrients all the way. Canned products are convenient and belong in every pantry. Without canned tomatoes and beans, being a vegetarian would be a lot tougher. The most important thing is to eat more vegetables and fruits and a greater variety of them.

Give Me Some Skin

Drop that peeler! The skin is often the most nutritious part of a vegetable. There's really no need to eliminate the peel on a potato, a summer squash or even a carrot unless it's really thick or the vegetable is bruised. Just scrub well and enjoy.

Shopping for Fresh Produce

Most of us shop for family meals in a supermarket and we're always looking for the best prices. Produce departments offer a huge selection of veggies and fruits and the good news is that often the biggest bargain is also the best choice. What's on sale is usually what's in season and that's tops for nutrition and taste. Flavor and texture vary depending on the freshness of the vegetable, how it was handled, what variety it is, how it was grown and even the soil it was grown in. Often commercial growers pick the varieties that are easiest to ship, last the longest or look prettiest. This does not always result in the best taste. Don't just choose the biggest, shiniest item in the bin. Feel it for firmness and rely on your sense of smell, too. A simple sniff of a melon or tomato can reveal a great deal.

"When I started cooking for myself, I realized that I didn't like buying, handling or preparing meat, so I probably shouldn't be eating it. That was 20 years ago. My meals are always colorful and delicious and nothing seems to be missing."

—Susie Brooke

The growth of farmers' markets has made vegetarian shopping a lot more fun. Make time to explore a market near you. Farmers and fellow shoppers will often be happy to share preparation tips and recipes. Ethnic markets are another great source for produce. Frequently stores that cater to Latin American, Italian, Asian or other clientele offer a wider selection and better prices. You'll be surprised at how many delicious kinds of eggplant there are that don't show up in an ordinary supermarket.

Keeping It Fresh

Most, but not all, fresh produce lasts longer if stored in the refrigerator. The vegetable crisper drawer is designed is to keep in humidity and protect veggies from the drier refrigerator air. Newer fridges often have a sliding tab on the front of the drawers that allows you to make further adjustments. Fruits usually require less humidity than vegetables.

Some fruits produce ethylene gas as they ripen. These include apples, avocados, bananas, peaches, plums, melons and tomatoes. Some vegetables are sensitive to ethylene and will spoil more quickly if exposed to it. Lettuce gets brown spots and broccoli buds may turn yellow. Be careful to keep the ethylene-producing fruits separate from broccoli, leafy greens, beans, carrots, cucumbers, eggplant, peas and peppers.

For maximum storage time, it's best to store produce unwashed. On the other hand, if you know you won't find the time during a busy workweek, fill the sink with water and take care of a big load all at once. Prepping vegetables ahead sometimes also makes sense. They won't keep as long, but you may be more likely to enjoy a pasta and veggie dinner if you can get it on the table faster. If you do prep before refrigerating, drain the produce well and store it in a plastic bag, preferably perforated. Add some paper towels to absorb any excess moisture. See the chart on the next page for more storage and freshness information.

COOL Labeling

As of 2008, retailers are required by law to indicate what country the produce they sell came from. The law is called COOL, which stands for Country Of Origin Labeling. So now you can choose to buy apples from the U.S. or avoid garlic from China. Pretty cool, isn't it?

"I renounced my carnivore vows three years ago, not because my mind said to do it, but my body was begging for salads with a veggie chaser."
—Su Bermingham

VEGETABLE	HOW TO STORE	USE WITHIN...
Artichokes	refrigerate, wrapped	7 days
Asparagus	refrigerate, wrap stalks in damp towel or place in glass with water	3 to 4 days
Beans, green snap, wax	refrigerate, unwashed in plastic bag	3 to 5 days
Beets	refrigerate, unwashed in plastic bag	2 weeks
Bell peppers, whole	refrigerate in crisper in plastic bag	1 to 2 weeks
Broccoli	refrigerate, unwashed in plastic bag	3 to 5 days
Cabbage	refrigerate, unwashed in plastic bag	1 to 2 weeks
Carrots, unpeeled	remove tops; refrigerate in plastic bag	3 to 4 weeks
Carrots, peeled and/or cut up, "baby" carrots	refrigerate, wrapped tightly in covered container	2 to 3 weeks
Celery	refrigerate in plastic bag or covered container	1 to 2 weeks
Chili peppers	refrigerate in crisper in plastic bag	1 week
Corn on the cob	refrigerate, unhusked and uncovered	1 to 2 days
Cucumber	refrigerate, unwashed in plastic bag	1 week
Eggplant	refrigerate, unwashed, in plastic bag	5 to 7 days
Garlic, whole bulb	store, uncovered at cool room temperature	3 to 5 months
Greens, salad	refrigerate, unwashed, in plastic bag	up to 1 week
Greens: kale, collards	refrigerate, unwashed, in plastic bag	5 days
Mushrooms, whole	refrigerate, unwashed, in *paper* bag	4 to 5 days
Mushrooms, sliced	refrigerate in covered container	1 to 2 days
Onions, whole	store in cool (50–60°F), dark place or refrigerate; do not store near potatoes*	2 to 3 months
Peas	refrigerate, unshelled, in plastic bag	3 to 5 days
Potatoes	store in cool (50–60°F), dark place; do not store near onions*	2 to 3 months
Spinach	refrigerate, unwashed, in plastic bag	3 to 5 days
Squash, summer	refrigerate, unwashed in plastic bag	4 to 5 days
Squash, winter	store in cool (50–60°F), dry place	1 to 2 months
Sweet potatoes	store in cool (50–60°F), dark place	1 month
Tomatoes	store at room temperature	1 to 5 days

Never store potatoes near onions. It speeds spoilage of both due to a chemical reaction between them.

The Well-Equipped Vegetarian

Knife Know-How

It's not that vegetarian cooking is different, but there are certain tools that can make it more enjoyable. (With what you're saving on groceries, you're entitled to treat yourself!) A sharp knife is the foundation of every good cook's kitchen kit. It makes chopping and slicing easier and neater and it's also safer. A dull knife is more likely to slip. Sharp knives slide through vegetables without crushing them and this can actually improve flavor and texture, too. If you've ever pulsed an onion for a bit too long in a food processor only to have it turn to watery mush, you get the idea.

Choosing the right knife has been the subject of many articles and you can easily do some research to understand the details we don't have room to handle here. The simplest rule, and one that is often overlooked, is that it's important to hold a knife to see how it fits in your hand and get a feel for weight and balance. A good knife should be an extension of the cook's hand.

It's just as important to keep your knives sharp as it is to buy good ones. Many hardware and cooking supply stores will sharpen your knives for a small fee. You can also buy an electric or manual sharpener to use at home. The steel (a metal rod mounted on a handle) is used to maintain the edge of your knives, but cannot actually sharpen them once they become dull. There's no need to have dozens of different knives. A good chef's knife, paring knife and a serrated knife (for tomatoes and bread) can handle just about any job.

"I was able to make the switch because I felt like I could not eat meat and still get a variety of flavors and dishes. Some people think the vegetarian diet consists of pizza, cheese and pasta constantly. This is not the case!"
—Michael Rice

A Washday Miracle!

One of the most time-consuming chores for the vegetarian cook is washing vegetables and the peskiest things to clean are greens like spinach and lettuce. Grit can hide in the leaves unless they are thoroughly swished underwater. Invest in a salad spinner if you haven't already. They come in a variety of styles, including those with a push-button or pull-string for spinning. Fill the sink with water, put the greens in the basket and swish away. Lift the basket out of the sink and spin dry, leaving dirt and grit behind.

Power on Tap

The vegetarian kitchen makes good use of food processors and blenders. They make shredding cabbage for a salad, puréeing a soup or preparing pesto a breeze. In addition to a full-size processor, a mini with only a one- or two-cup capacity can be handy for small amounts of veggies, herbs or nuts. A blender is a must if you make smoothies, and it can also make creamy dips, soups and sauces. An immersion blender (the kind that you stick into the pot) is not as powerful but can be useful if you make a lot of soups; you won't have to transfer hot liquid to and from a regular blender or processor.

Pots, Pans, Skillets, Etc.

A big (2-gallon) stockpot will serve you well for making soup, blanching vegetables and cooking pasta. You'll also need a large ovenproof Dutch oven or deep skillet with a lid for making stews and braising. A small and/or medium saucepan can take care of steaming or boiling. You'll need small and medium skillets for sautéing as well as a large (12-inch) deep skillet for preparing stir-fries, one-dish meals and large quantities of vegetables.

For use in the oven, a large metal roasting pan and a rimmed baking sheet (sometimes called a jelly-roll pan) are the minimum. You probably already have an assortment of smaller baking dishes and casseroles. It's nice to have a gratin dish and a soufflé dish as well, though a casserole can usually fill in.

A large cutting board is essential—at least 10×12 inches. Smaller boards are frustrating. They don't give you room to safely chop an entire bunch of parsley or an eggplant without things falling off the edges. It's best to have more than one cutting board so you don't have to keep washing and drying between tasks. Plastic has the advantage of usually being dishwasher safe, but wood boards are also a fine choice. If the board slides around while you're working, anchor it by placing a damp towel underneath.

If you enjoy grilling, it's worth investing in a vegetable grill basket or grill-topper. These useful tools allow you to grill small items or small pieces of larger ones without anything falling through the grate. A perforated metal steamer that fits inside a saucepan or an Asian bamboo steamer can also come in handy.

Beyond Broccoli

Most folks who say they can't imagine what vegetarians eat lack imagination themselves! The plant kingdom offers choices of color, texture and taste that go way beyond the dull beige world of meat. Nevertheless, it is easy to get stuck in a rut and keep repeating the same old broccoli, corn and zucchini. Here are some ideas for moving beyond the usual veggie rotation.

Artichokes

Fresh artichokes' peak season is the early spring. In addition to the familiar globe artichoke, you will sometimes see fresh baby artichokes. They usually don't have a choke that has to be removed and they are tender enough to cook quickly. Frozen and canned artichoke hearts are excellent items to have on hand. Jarred marinated hearts are packed in oil and add a different flavor to dishes.

Bok choy and other Asian greens

In Chinese the word "choy" means greens. Bok choy with crisp white stalks and dark green leaves is the most common. What is sometimes labeled baby bok choy is a miniature jade green variety. There is also choy sum (white flowering cabbage). They all have a mild cabbage flavor and can be used interchangeably with each other and in other cabbage recipes, so don't hesitate to try something new.

Chayote and other summer squash

There are dozens of kinds of summer squash besides zucchini. Chayote, which is sometimes called mirliton, is light green and pear-shaped. The flavor is mild and a bit sweet. Even the stone in the center is edible (and delicious). There are also pattypan squash, which look like cute flying saucers, and a round zucchini-like squash sometimes labeled "8 ball squash." All of these can be used interchangeably although cooking times will need to be adjusted.

Chard

Sometimes called *Swiss chard*, this gorgeous "green" comes in a rainbow of hues. Stems can be thick or thin, red, yellow or white. It is related to beets and spinach and tastes a bit like both. Stems take longer to cook than the leaves, so give them a head start.

Eggplant

If you are only familiar with the big purple globe eggplant available year round, you're in for a treat. Check a farmers' market or ethnic produce department in the summer and you'll find a huge variety. Slender Asian eggplants are shades of purple or striped with white. There are egg-size white eggplants—yes, that's where the name came from—and even reddish orange and pale green varieties. In season, eggplant should have firm flesh with very little in the way of developed seeds. There's no need to peel or salt most varieties since they won't have the bitterness that puts some people off.

Fennel

Crisp, juicy fennel is an Italian vegetable that is finally being appreciated here. You will also see fennel labeled "finocchio" or "anise." Fennel can be enjoyed raw and sliced thin in a salad. Cooked, fennel's flavor mellows and sweetens. Add fennel to pasta dishes and mixed roasted vegetables.

Leeks

They look like green onions on steroids, but leeks, although related to onions, can play a different leading role. Once cooked, leeks soften and add sweet complexity to soups, stews, casseroles and other dishes. It is crucial to clean leeks thoroughly since mud hides deep between the leaves. Make sure to slit the leek horizontally and swish under copious amounts of water until the water runs clear.

Mushrooms

Pity the poor white button mushroom, which has now been upstaged by so many other tasty varieties. The brown *cremini* is actually the same type of mushroom as the white, just a different strain. And a *cremini* left to mature to its full adult size is the much-loved *portobello*. Shiitake mushrooms are now available fresh. The dried *shiitake*, also called Chinese black mushroom, is most likely familiar to anyone who has dined in a Chinese restaurant. Fresh *shiitakes* offer a milder version of the rich, meaty flavor of dried. Seek out those with thick, firm caps and a fresh aroma. *Oyster mushrooms* grow in thick clusters with overlapping leaflike caps. Their flavor is mild and their texture slightly chewy. You will often find a mix of the mushrooms just described packaged together and labeled "wild mushrooms." They are, almost always, not truly wild, but cultivated versions of what exists in the wild. This is a good thing since they are much less expensive and also safer than mushrooms that have been foraged.

Root vegetables

Root veggies won't win any beauty contests, but what they lack in looks they more than make up in flavor. Roasted or braised, they turn soft and seductive. The two most popular roots—carrots and potatoes—are regulars in most kitchens, but there are many delicious options to explore.

Celery root may be the ugliest of the bunch. This large gnarly bulb, which is also called celeriac or knob celery, has a tough exterior covered in deep furrows. Don't try to peel celery root with an ordinary peeler; remove its outer shell with a paring knife. It can be used in gratins, mashed with potatoes, roasted or even used raw for a famous French café slaw: celeri remoulade. The flavor is like celery, only deeper.

Rutabagas look like bigger, brawnier turnips and are related. Their exteriors are dark yellow with a purple blush and are often heavily waxed to keep them fresh. Inside, a rutabaga's flesh is a pale yellow. Like turnips, rutabagas are tastiest when young and not too big. Extra large rutabagas are carved into jack-o'-lanterns for Halloween in England and Ireland. *Kohlrabi* is actually a member of the cabbage family. The golf to tennis ball-size bulbs are pale green or purple outside. The flesh is crisp and has a broccoli-like flavor. Enjoy kohlrabi raw, or prepare it steamed, sauteed or roasted to bring out its sweetness.

If it looks like a carrot only white, it's probably a *parsnip*. These delicious roots may be the most under appreciated of all. Steamed, braised, roasted or pureed, parsnips are low in calories and high in fiber and have a light, earthy sweetness. Their flavor is even sweeter when they're harvested after a frost.

Winter squash

From the large *butternut* to the diminutive *delicata*, winter squash come in a boggling array of sizes and colors. Aside from Halloween pumpkins (good for toasted seeds and jack-o'-lanterns, but not for cooking), the largest variety that is readily available and offers good flavor is the smooth, beige *butternut squash*. This slightly sweet, rich tasting squash is classic in almost any preparation from soup to risotto. *Delicata squash* has recently become available and can be used like the more common acorn. This green-striped oblong squash cooks up tender with a buttery texture and a flavor reminiscent of corn. *Spaghetti squash* is like no other. It looks like a rounded golden football and when cooked yields crisp-tender strands that look like, and can be sauced like, you guessed it, spaghetti!

Going with the Grain

Grains are the center of the plate in many cultures. Asian cuisine is built around rice. In Thailand the traditional greeting translates as, "Have you eaten rice yet?" Italy has pasta made from durum wheat. In both North and South America, corn was central to ancient cuisine and culture. Bread and cereal are certainly mainstays of our lives, but fortunately there are more kinds of grains now available than ever and there are delicious options that go way beyond a loaf of white bread.

Storing Grains

Whole grains are considerably more nutritious than processed ones, but since they contain the oil-rich germ as well as the bran, they become rancid much more quickly. It's best to store what you won't use up in several months in the refrigerator or freezer. Buy small quantities of an assortment of grains and keep them in covered containers labeled with the date they were purchased. If you are buying from bulk bins, take a good sniff first. Grain should smell sweet and earthy not stale or rancid. Grains that are past their prime not only don't taste good, they take longer to cook.

barley

Slightly sweet, nutty and chewy, barley is easy to love and makes a good substitute for rice. Pearl (pearled) barley, which is the most available kind, has been polished to remove its tough outer hull. Hulled or Scotch barley has more of the bran intact so is more nutritious but also takes longer to cook.

> ### The Kernel of the Matter
>
> All grains have three parts. There is a tough outer layer that protects the grain called the bran. The starchy endosperm makes up the biggest portion of the kernel. The germ or the embryo of the grain is at its base. The bran and the germ contain the most fiber and nutrients; they are the parts often removed when grain is processed. Whole grains still contain all three parts.

Polenta Lasagna, pg. 140

bulgur wheat

To make bulgur wheat, whole kernels are steamed, dried and ground to varying degrees. The fine grind, which is the most common type, is ready in a matter of minutes. Bulgur is traditionally served cold in tabbouleh salad, but its fluffy texture also makes it a natural for soaking up juices or broths.

cornmeal/polenta

Polenta is the Italian name for a creamy porridge made from cornmeal that is eaten hot or cooled, sliced and fried. The American version of this dish would be called cornmeal mush. It's easy to see why it never caught on under that name! Polenta is most nutritious and flavorful if prepared from whole grain, stone-ground cornmeal.

couscous

We call couscous a grain, but it's actually a form of tiny pasta made from wheat flour. Whole wheat couscous is just as convenient as regular since it cooks in the same amount of time.

millet

Mild-mannered millet has small beadlike grains that cook quickly. Once considered "for the birds", millet is being recognized for its pleasant cornlike flavor and good nutritional profile—millet is rich in B vitamins.

quinoa

If you're only going to add one new grain to your meals, make it quinoa. The Incas considered it sacred and called it the mother of all grains. Quinoa has also been called a supergrain since it is rich in protein, contains all essential amino acids, and is a good source of fiber, magnesium and iron. Oh, yes, it is also easy to digest, has a sweet subtle taste and cooks in about 15 minutes!

> ## Grains as Convenience Foods
>
> It's true that whole grains take time to cook, but there's an easy way to enjoy them even on a busy weeknight. Stockpile! Instead of preparing just 1 cup of rice, barley, quinoa or whatever, double or triple the recipe and store the rest. Cooked grains will keep for several days in the refrigerator and for months in the freezer.

rice

Brown rice is whole grain rice with the nutrients in the bran or germ intact. There are many varieties of rice and they are often categorized by the length of their grains. *Long-grain rice* is at least three times longer than it is wide. These rices include the aromatic *jasmine* and *basmati* rices. *Short-grain rice* has plumper, rounder grains that tend to stick together more when cooked. Sushi rice and arborio rice are two examples. Rice that is especially sticky is often used in Asian desserts and is sometimes labeled *sweet or glutinous rice*, despite the fact that it contains no gluten!

wheat berries

These kernels of wheat are sold under the name whole wheat or wheat berries. The color of the berries (which are actually kernels) varies from reddish brown to pale cream. Wheat berries have a hearty, nutty flavor and satisfying chewiness. They can take up to an hour to cook, but the time can be shortened by presoaking.

> ## Five Ways to Enjoy Leftover Grain
>
> *1.* Add a cup of cooked grain to a muffin or bread recipe.
>
> *2.* Add cooked grains to soups.
>
> *3.* Make a cold salad by adding colorful veggies and fruits to cooked grain.
>
> *4.* Shape leftover rice, quinoa or bulgur wheat into croquettes with the addition of egg and seasoning. Pan fry.
>
> *5.* Try leftover rice, quinoa or millet for breakfast with fruit, cinnamon and sugar.

The Beauty of Beans

Beans are one of the least expensive forms of protein. They are high in fiber and low in fat and come in a kaleidoscope of colors and shapes. Beans can be enjoyed in every kind of dish from a dip or a salad to stews and soups to hearty main courses. In Asia, sweetened red beans are dessert—they are used to fill pastries and even make ice cream!

adzuki beans
These small, dark red beans are slightly sweet and creamy when cooked. They are the basis for sweet red bean paste used in Asian desserts.

black beans (turtle beans, frijoles negros)
Black beans are a staple of Latin American dishes. Their strong, earthy flavor and firm texture help them stand out in soups, salads and all sorts of side dishes.

cannellini beans (white kidney beans)
Mild-tasting meaty cannellinis are often used in minestrone soup and other Italian dishes.

chickpeas (garbanzo beans)
The versatile chickpea has an almost buttery flavor and is a nutritional powerhouse with over 80 nutrients, plus plenty of fiber and protein. Many classic vegetarian dishes, including hummus and falafel, are based on the versatile chickpea.

kidney beans
Kidney beans are full-flavored and retain their kidney shape even with long cooking times. They are usually the bean of choice for chili or cold salads. They come in dark red, light red, pink or white (see cannellini beans).

lentils
Lentils cook quickly and are often served puréed. The most common varieties are brown and red, but for a larger selection explore the many different kinds used in Indian or Middle Eastern cuisines.

lima beans (butter beans)
Pale green limas are starchy and satisfying. If you've only had canned, give them another chance. Their rich buttery flavor holds up better when they're fresh or frozen.

pinto beans
Speckled beige beans with darker streaks, pintos are used for refried beans, chili and many Mexican recipes. Unfortunately their pretty markings—"pinto" means painted in Spanish—turn a dull pinkish beige after cooking.

white beans (Great Northern, navy beans)
These mild, meaty beans are favorites in casseroles, stews and soups.

What's the difference between a bean and a legume?

Legumes are a class of vegetable that includes beans, peas and lentils, all of which grow in pods. What about green beans? When the entire pod is eaten, the plant is considered a green vegetable.

Dry Bean Basics

Cooking dried beans is easy, economical and produces firmer, tastier beans. It does take more time than opening a can, but most of it is unsupervised.

1. Buy the right beans. Old beans or those that have been stored in heat or humidity will never cook correctly. (Throw away that old package that's been in your cupboard for five years right now!) Purchase beans from a place that has a big turnover. Choose beans that are brightly colored with smooth skins.

2. Soak. Sort through the beans and discard any broken ones or foreign matter while rinsing them thoroughly. Place in a nonreactive bowl or pan and cover with fresh cold water by about 3 inches. Toss any beans that float. Soak at least four hours or overnight until the bean skins get wrinkled. (There is no need to soak lentils.)

3. Cook. Drain the beans and rinse them. Place them in a saucepan and cover with at least one inch of water. Bring the beans to a boil and skim any foam that rises to the top. Cover and simmer the beans over low heat for 45 minutes to 2 hours or until tender but not mushy. Timing will depend on the variety of bean and also how long it was stored. Add hot water if needed to keep the beans covered. Add salt and seasonings when the beans are almost tender.

> "When I was 13 years old, I looked at a piece of meat and couldn't eat it. I saw the animal on the plate in front of me. Every since then I've been a vegetarian."
> —Abby Rubenstein

Barley, Bean and Corn Frittata, pg. 156

Black Bean and Mushroom Chilaquiles, pg. 166

Bean Counting

One pound of dried beans will yield four to five cups of cooked beans, or approximately 8 servings. A 15-ounce can contains between 1½ to 2 cups of cooked beans, depending on the variety.

Using Your Noodles

Pasta may be a vegetarian's best friend! It's economical, versatile and easy to prepare. You can stuff it, sauce it, stir-fry it, bake it or make it into a fried cake. You can buy it dried in a box, fresh and in more shapes and colors than we have room for here. Besides Italian pasta, there are dozens of kinds of Asian noodles. Some are practically identical to their Italian counterparts. Others are made of different ingredients and require different cooking methods. Whatever your favorites, there's no such thing as too much noodling around!

Does shape matter?

That depends on the recipe and your personal preferences. Obviously you wouldn't try to make lasagna with elbow macaroni. Although if you layered the cooked elbows with sauce and cheese, you'd end up with something delicious— it just wouldn't be called lasagna! Common sense and tradition indicate that a chunky sauce works better if there's a shape to catch it, like shells or orecchiette. For a soup, you need a shape that fits into a spoon. And for stuffing you need a shape that's big enough to fit a spoon in!

Umami: The Fifth Flavor

In addition to sweet, sour, salty and bitter, there is a taste that can be described as savoriness or meatiness. Called "umami" from the Japanese, this taste is present in meat, but also in mushrooms, soy sauce and other fermented soy products, cheese, ripe tomatoes, wine and balsamic vinegar. To add full-bodied savor to vegetarian dishes, add umami ingredients.

ASIAN NOODLES

Soba noodles are flat Japanese noodles made with buckwheat flour, which gives them an earthy, nutty flavor. They are served cold during hot Japanese summers and hot in winter soups. Soba should be cooked until tender, not al dente.

Rice noodles come in a dizzying array of sizes and go by a number of names—rice sticks and rice vermicelli are two. Unlike soba or pasta, rice noodles only need to be soaked in hot water before using.

Chinese wheat noodles (mein) are similar to pasta and come in just as many styles and shapes with or without the addition of egg. They are cooked like pasta, too, and you can substitute a similar pasta shape if you have trouble finding the real thing.

Rice papers are translucent round sheets made from rice flour and water. They need only to be soaked for 20 seconds before being used to wrap ingredients. See the recipe for Vegetarian Summer Rolls on page 84.

The Pasta Cooking Quiz

There is a lot written about the simple art of cooking pasta, some of it contradictory. Test your knowledge with this quiz.

1. **What's the best way to cook pasta?**

a. Place it in several quarts of cold water and bring to a boil.

b. Add pasta to boiling water, add salt and cover the pot.

c. Bring an abundant quantity of salted water to a boil. Add pasta, stir and boil uncovered.

2. **How much salt should you add to pasta water?**

a. None. Pasta should be salted after cooking.

b. Two teaspoons

c. Enough to make it taste like the sea.

3. **You should add a tablespoon of olive oil to pasta cooking water...**

a. if you're worried about the pasta sticking together.

b. if you will be using a low-fat sauce.

c. Never!

4. **How do you tell when pasta is done?**

a. You follow the directions on the box and add a few minutes.

b. You throw it against the wall and see if it sticks.

c. You taste it.

5. **What does al dente mean?**

a. Pasta shaped like little teeth.

b. It's a small town in the Italian hills known for great pasta.

c. Literally "to the tooth." It's a description of perfectly cooked pasta that retains a little bite, but is not chalky in the middle.

Spinach Stuffed Manicotti, pg.126

ANSWERS: Every correct answer is letter "c."

Tofu and Friends

Sometimes tofu, seitan and tempeh are referred to as meat substitutes. It's true that these ingredients can be made into shapes that resemble meat and they have a satisfying chew and somewhat meaty flavor. However, many vegetarians enjoy them because they are delicious and nutritious in and of themselves.

You probably know that tofu is made from soybeans, but you may be unaware that the process that produces it is very similar to making cheese. A salt- or acid-based coagulant is added to soymilk to form curds and whey. (Remember Little Miss Muffet?) Once the curds are drained and pressed you have a block of tofu. While tofu is a relatively recent addition to American kitchens, it has been a huge part of Asian cuisine for centuries.

Buying and Storing Tofu

Tofu comes in many forms as a visit to any Asian market will illustrate, but there are two main types. *Regular or brick tofu* (sometimes called *Chinese tofu*) is sold in the refrigerated section of the supermarket in the produce section or near the dairy case and comes sealed in a plastic tub filled with water. There is usually a choice of soft, medium, firm or extra-firm. Once opened, regular tofu will keep in the refrigerator up to 4 days. The water should be drained and replaced daily.

Pressing Tofu

It isn't absolutely necessary, but pressing tofu removes excess moisture, which makes the tofu easier to handle and allows it to absorb flavors better. To press tofu, you need to make a sort of tofu sandwich. Place it on a cutting board or plate lined with a paper towels. Cover with more paper towels and place a flat, heavy object, like a saucepan on top. Press the tofu for 15 minutes or more. Drain excess moisture as needed.

Silken tofu, sometimes called *Japanese tofu*, is the sort that comes in an aseptic box, which does not require refrigeration. While it also comes in soft, medium or firm, the texture of silken tofu is almost custard-like compared to regular. It is an excellent thickener and works well in soups. Silken tofu is too delicate to use in most stir-fries where it will crumble and dissolve.

Tempeh

Tempeh (pronounced "tem-pay") is a very nutritious fermented soy food that originated in Indonesia hundreds of years ago. Although it won't win prizes for good

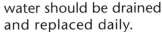

Teriyaki Tempeh with Pineapple, pg. 82

looks—it looks like a messy cake of beans and nuts squashed together—tempeh has a nutty, yeasty flavor and chewy texture that is easy to learn to love. You'll find cakes of tempeh, vacuum-packed and refrigerated, in natural food stores and some supermarkets. Soybean tempeh is the classic version, but tempeh can also be made of rice and other grains, or be a mixture of soy and grain.

Using Tempeh

It's best to cook tempeh before eating it, although this is for taste reasons rather than food safety ones. Cooking improves both flavor and texture. Like tofu, tempeh has an ability to readily absorb flavors and cooking enhances this. Its firm texture makes it a great choice to replace ground beef, cook on the grill or use in a sandwich.

Seitan

Seiten (pronounced "say-tan") is sometimes called wheat-meat, gluten-meat or mock duck. It is made from wheat by washing away the starch component until only the wheat protein—gluten—is left. If you've ever eaten mock duck or mock chicken in a Chinese restaurant, you've tried seitan. It is also the base for some commercial vegetarian deli "meats."

Using Seitan

You'll find seitan in the refrigerated or freezer section of natural food stores packed in a marinade in a tub or a vacuum pack. Varieties are flavored, Asian-style with soy and ginger, or seasoned to taste like chicken or other meat. Seitan is incredibly versatile. It can be stir-fried, baked, broiled or grilled.

Thai Seitan Stir-Fry, pg. 86

"I became a vegetarian in college when I realized that I just don't like the texture of meat and the thought of where it comes from makes me squeamish. I've been vegetarian for 12 years and I love it. I'm less picky and more adventurous than I used to be as an omnivore."

—Carissa Kinyon

Souper Bowls

Zesty Vegetarian Chili

1 tablespoon vegetable oil

1 large red bell pepper, coarsely chopped

2 medium zucchini or yellow squash (or 1 of each), cut into chunks

4 cloves garlic, minced

1 can (about 14 ounces) fire-roasted diced tomatoes

¾ cup chunky salsa

2 teaspoons chili powder

1 teaspoon dried oregano

1 can (about 15 ounces) red kidney beans, rinsed and drained

10 ounces extra-firm tofu, drained and cut into cubes

Chopped fresh cilantro (optional)

1. Heat oil in large saucepan over medium heat. Add bell pepper; cook and stir 4 minutes. Add zucchini and garlic; cook and stir 3 minutes.

2. Stir in tomatoes, salsa, chili powder and oregano; bring to a boil over high heat. Reduce heat; simmer 15 minutes or until vegetables are tender.

3. Stir beans into chili. Simmer 2 minutes or until heated through. Stir in tofu; remove from heat. Ladle into shallow bowls; garnish with chopped cilantro, if desired.

Makes 4 servings

Oven-Roasted Beet Soup with Orange Cream

½ **cup sour cream**

1 **teaspoon grated orange peel**

1 **tablespoon packed brown sugar**

1 **tablespoon orange juice**

1 **bunch beets (4 to 6), peeled and diced (about 4 cups)**

1 **pound parsnips, diced**

1 **medium sweet onion, chopped (about 1 cup)**

2 **cloves garlic, sliced**

2 **tablespoons olive oil**

5 **cups SWANSON® Vegetable Broth (Regular or Certified Organic)**

1. Stir the sour cream, ½ **teaspoon** of the orange peel, brown sugar and orange juice in a small bowl. Cover and refrigerate.

2. Heat the oven to 425°F. Spread the beets, parsnips, onion and garlic in a single layer in a 17×11-inch roasting pan. Pour the oil over the vegetables and toss to coat. Season to taste. Bake for 25 minutes or until the beets are tender.

3. Place **half** of the vegetable mixture and ½ **cup** of the broth and remaining orange peel into an electric blender or food processor container. Cover and blend until smooth. Pour the puréed mixture into a 3-quart saucepan. Repeat the blending process with the remaining vegetables and ½ **cup** broth. Add to the saucepan with the remaining broth. Cook over high heat to a boil. Reduce the heat to low. Cook for 10 minutes.

4. Divide the soup among **6** serving bowls and top **each** with **about 1 tablespoon** of the sour cream mixture. *Makes 6 servings*

Prep Time: 20 minutes
Cook Time: 35 minutes

Bean Ragoût with Cilantro-Cornmeal Dumplings

1 tablespoon vegetable oil

2 large onions, chopped

1 poblano pepper, seeded and chopped

3 cloves garlic, minced

3 tablespoons chili powder

2 teaspoons ground cumin

1 teaspoon dried oregano

1 can (28 ounces) whole tomatoes, undrained, chopped

2 small zucchini, cut into ½-inch pieces

2 cups chopped red bell peppers

1 can (about 15 ounces) pinto beans, rinsed and drained

1 can (about 15 ounces) black beans, rinsed and drained

¾ teaspoon salt, divided

Black pepper

½ cup all-purpose flour

½ cup cornmeal

1 teaspoon baking powder

2 tablespoons shortening

¼ cup (1 ounce) shredded Cheddar cheese

1 tablespoon minced fresh cilantro

½ cup milk

1. Heat oil in Dutch oven over medium heat. Add onions; cook and stir 5 minutes or until tender. Add poblano pepper, garlic, chili powder, cumin and oregano; cook and stir 1 to 2 minutes.

2. Add tomatoes with juice, zucchini, bell peppers, beans and ¼ teaspoon salt; bring to a boil. Reduce heat to medium-low. Simmer 5 to 10 minutes or until zucchini is tender. Season with salt and black pepper.

3. To prepare dumplings, combine flour, cornmeal, baking powder and remaining ½ teaspoon salt in medium bowl. Cut in shortening with pastry blender or two knives until mixture resembles coarse crumbs.

4. Stir in cheese and cilantro. Add milk; stir just until dry ingredients are moistened.

5. Drop dumpling dough into six mounds on top of simmering ragoût. Cook, uncovered, 5 minutes. Cover; cook 5 to 10 minutes or until toothpick inserted into dumplings comes out clean.   *Makes 6 servings*

Carrot Soup

2 teaspoons butter
⅓ cup chopped onion
1 tablespoon chopped fresh ginger
1 pound baby carrots
½ teaspoon salt
¼ teaspoon black pepper
3 cups vegetable broth
¼ cup whipping cream
¼ cup orange juice
   Pinch ground nutmeg
4 tablespoons sour cream

1. Melt butter in large saucepan over medium-high heat. Add onion and ginger; cook and stir 1 minute or until ginger is fragrant. Add carrots, salt and pepper; cook and stir 2 minutes.

2. Stir in broth; bring to a boil. Reduce heat to medium-low; cover and simmer 30 minutes or until carrots are tender.

3. Working in batches, process soup in blender or food processor until smooth. Return to saucepan; stir in cream, orange juice and nutmeg. Cook over medium heat until heated through, stirring occasionally. Thin soup with additional broth, if necessary. Top soup with sour cream just before serving. *Makes 4 servings*

Vegan Variation: Replace butter with vegetable oil and omit whipping cream and sour cream.

White Bean & Escarole Soup

1½ cups dried baby lima beans or butter beans, rinsed and sorted
1 teaspoon olive oil
½ cup chopped celery
⅓ cup coarsely chopped onion
2 cloves garlic, minced
1 can (28 ounces) whole tomatoes, undrained, chopped
½ cup chopped fresh parsley
2 tablespoons chopped fresh rosemary leaves
¼ teaspoon black pepper
1 head escarole, shredded

1. Place dried lima beans and water to cover by several inches in large bowl. Soak 6 to 8 hours or overnight. Drain beans; place in large saucepan or Dutch oven. Cover with water; bring to a boil over high heat. Reduce heat to low. Cover and simmer about 1 hour or until tender. Drain.

2. Meanwhile, heat oil in small skillet over medium heat. Add celery, onion and garlic; cook and stir 5 minutes or until onion is tender.

3. Add celery mixture and tomatoes with juice to beans. Stir in parsley, rosemary and pepper. Cover and simmer over low heat 15 minutes. Add escarole; simmer 5 minutes or until wilted.

Makes 6 servings

Tip Escarole is a green that is usually used in salads. It has broad green leaves that look a bit like a curlier version of romaine lettuce and is part of the endive family. White Bean and Escarole Soup is a classic Italian preparation which is often made with cannellini beans. Canned cannellini beans may be substituted in this recipe, if desired.

Gazpacho

6 large very ripe tomatoes (about 3 pounds), divided
1½ cups tomato juice
1 clove garlic
2 tablespoons fresh lime juice
2 tablespoons olive oil
1 tablespoon white wine vinegar
1 teaspoon sugar
½ to 1 teaspoon salt
½ teaspoon dried oregano
6 green onions, sliced
¼ cup finely chopped celery
¼ cup finely chopped seeded cucumber
1 or 2 fresh jalapeño peppers,* minced
   Garlic Croutons (page 37) or packaged croutons
1 cup diced avocado
1 red or green bell pepper, chopped
2 tablespoons chopped fresh cilantro

Jalapeño peppers can sting and irritate the skin, so wear rubber gloves when handling peppers and do not touch your eyes.

1. Seed and finely chop 1 tomato; set aside.

2. Coarsely chop remaining 5 tomatoes; process half of tomatoes, ¾ cup tomato juice and garlic in blender until smooth. Press through sieve into large bowl; discard seeds. Repeat with remaining coarsely chopped tomatoes and ¾ cup tomato juice.

3. Whisk lime juice, oil, vinegar, sugar, salt and oregano into tomato mixture. Stir in finely chopped tomato, green onions, celery, cucumber and jalapeños. Cover; refrigerate at least 4 hours or up to 24 hours to develop flavors.

4. Prepare Garlic Croutons.

5. Stir soup; ladle into chilled bowls. Top with croutons, avocado, bell pepper and cilantro. *Makes 4 servings*

Garlic Croutons

5 slices firm white bread
2 tablespoons olive oil
1 clove garlic, minced
¼ teaspoon paprika

1. Preheat oven to 300°F. Trim crusts from bread; cut into ½-inch cubes.

2. Heat oil in skillet over medium heat. Stir in garlic and paprika. Add bread; cook and stir 1 minute or just until bread is evenly coated with oil.

3. Spread bread on baking sheet. Bake 20 to 25 minutes until crisp and golden. Cool.

Makes about 2 cups

Jamaican Black Bean Stew

    2 pounds sweet potatoes
    3 pounds butternut squash
    1 large onion, coarsely chopped
    1 can (about 14 ounces) vegetable broth
    3 cloves garlic, minced
    1 tablespoon curry powder
  1½ teaspoons ground allspice
    ½ teaspoon ground red pepper
    ¼ teaspoon salt
    2 cans (about 15 ounces each) black beans, rinsed and drained
    ½ cup raisins
    3 tablespoons fresh lime juice
    1 cup diced tomato
    1 cup diced peeled cucumber
       Cooked brown rice

1. Peel sweet potatoes; cut into ¾-inch chunks to measure about 4 cups. Peel squash; remove seeds. Cut flesh into ¾-inch cubes to measure about 5 cups.

2. Combine sweet potatoes, squash, onion, broth, garlic, curry powder, allspice, red pepper and salt in Dutch oven. Bring to a boil; reduce heat to low. Simmer, covered, 15 minutes or until sweet potatoes and squash are tender. Add beans and raisins. Simmer 5 minutes or until heated through. Remove from heat; stir in lime juice.

3. Serve stew over brown rice and top with tomato and cucumber.

Makes 8 servings

Chile Pepper & Corn Cream Chowder

2 tablespoons butter

1 cup chopped onion

2 Anaheim* or poblano chile peppers, diced

½ cup thinly sliced celery

1 package (16 ounces) frozen corn

12 ounces new red potatoes, diced

4 cups whole milk

6 ounces cream cheese, cubed

2 teaspoons salt

¾ teaspoon black pepper

Mild, with just the hint of a bite, Anaheim chiles are medium green peppers with a long narrow shape.

1. Melt butter in large saucepan over medium-high heat. Add onion, Anaheim peppers and celery; cook and stir 5 minutes or until onion is translucent.

2. Add corn, potatoes and milk. Bring to a boil. Reduce heat to medium-low; cover and simmer 10 minutes or until potatoes are tender.

3. Remove from heat; add cream cheese, salt and black pepper. Stir until cream cheese is melted. *Makes 4 to 6 servings*

Tip

Chile peppers come in a practically unlimited assortment of colors, sizes and degrees of heat. Anaheim peppers are named after the city in California. A red version of the Anaheim pepper is called chile Colorado. Poblano chile peppers have dark green, almost black, skins that are as shiny as patent leather. They are also fairly mild and are often used for stuffing. In their dried form, poblanos are called ancho chiles.

Spicy African Chickpea & Sweet Potato Stew

    Spice Paste (page 45)
1½ **pounds sweet potatoes, peeled and cubed**
  2 **cups vegetable broth or water**
  1 **can (16 ounces) plum tomatoes, undrained, chopped**
  1 **can (16 ounces) chickpeas, drained and rinsed**
1½ **cups sliced fresh okra** *or* **1 package (10 ounces) frozen cut okra, thawed**
    Yellow Couscous (recipe follows)
    Hot pepper sauce
    Fresh cilantro (optional)

1. Prepare Spice Paste.

2. Combine sweet potatoes, broth, tomatoes with juice, chickpeas, okra and Spice Paste in large saucepan. Bring to a boil over high heat. Reduce heat to low. Cover and simmer 15 minutes. Uncover; simmer 10 minutes or until vegetables are tender.

3. Meanwhile, prepare Yellow Couscous.

4. Serve stew with couscous and hot pepper sauce. Garnish with cilantro.

Makes 4 servings

Yellow Couscous

  1 **tablespoon olive oil**
  5 **green onions, sliced**
1⅔ **cups water**
  ⅛ **teaspoon saffron threads** *or* ½ **teaspoon ground turmeric**
  ¼ **teaspoon salt**
  1 **cup uncooked couscous**

Heat oil in medium saucepan over medium heat Add green onions; cook and stir 4 minutes. Add water, saffron and salt. Bring to a boil; stir in couscous. Remove from heat. Cover; let stand 5 minutes or until water is absorbed. Fluff couscous with fork.

Makes 3 cups

Spice Paste

6 cloves garlic, peeled
1 teaspoon coarse salt
2 teaspoons paprika
1½ teaspoons whole cumin seeds
1 teaspoon black pepper
½ teaspoon ground ginger
½ teaspoon ground allspice
1 tablespoon olive oil

Process garlic and salt in blender or small food processor until garlic is finely chopped. Add remaining seasonings. Process 15 seconds. With blender running, pour oil through cover opening; process until mixture forms paste.

Two-Cheese Potato & Cauliflower Soup

1 tablespoon butter

1 cup chopped onion

2 cloves garlic, minced

5 cups whole milk

1 pound Yukon Gold potatoes, diced

1 pound cauliflower florets

1½ teaspoons salt

⅛ teaspoon ground red pepper

1½ cups (6 ounces) shredded sharp Cheddar cheese

⅓ cup crumbled blue cheese

1. Melt butter in saucepan over medium-high heat. Add onion; cook and stir 4 minutes or until translucent. Add garlic; cook and stir 15 seconds. Add milk, potatoes, cauliflower, salt and red pepper; bring to a boil. Reduce heat; cover tightly and simmer 15 minutes or until potatoes are tender. Cool slightly.

2. Working in batches, process soup in blender or food processor until smooth. Return to saucepan. Cook and stir over medium heat 2 to 3 minutes or until heated through. Remove from heat; add cheeses. Stir until cheese are melted.

Makes 4 to 6 servings

Tip: One pound of trimmed cauliflower will yield about 1½ cups of florets. You can also substitute 1 pound of frozen cauliflower florets for the fresh florets.

Caribbean Sweet Potato & Bean Stew

2 medium sweet potatoes (about 1 pound), peeled and cut into 1-inch cubes

2 cups frozen cut green beans

1 can (about 15 ounces) black beans, rinsed and drained

1 can (about 14 ounces) vegetable broth

1 small onion, sliced

2 teaspoons Caribbean jerk seasoning

½ teaspoon dried thyme

¼ teaspoon salt

¼ teaspoon ground cinnamon

⅓ cup slivered almonds, toasted*

Hot pepper sauce (optional)

To toast almonds, spread in single layer on baking sheet. Bake in preheated 350°F oven 8 to 10 minutes or until golden brown, stirring frequently.

Slow Cooker Directions

1. Combine sweet potatoes, beans, broth, onion, jerk seasoning, thyme, salt and cinnamon in slow cooker. Cover; cook on LOW 5 to 6 hours or until vegetables are tender.

2. Serve with almonds and hot pepper sauce, if desired.   *Makes 4 servings*

Tip Sweet potatoes are high in vitamin A and C and rich in antioxidants. Dark fleshed sweet potatoes are sometimes called "yams", but true yams are not related. In fact, sweet potatoes aren't closely related to regular potatoes either! Choose sweet potatoes that are firm with unbruised skins. Store them in a cool, dry place—not the refrigerator.

Vegetable Minestrone Soup

2 tablespoons olive or vegetable oil
2 medium zucchini, cut in half lengthwise and thickly sliced (about 3 cups)
2 cloves garlic, minced
½ teaspoon dried rosemary leaves, crushed
4 cups SWANSON® Vegetable Broth (Regular or Certified Organic)
1 can (about 14½ ounces) diced tomatoes, drained
1 can (about 19 ounces) white kidney beans (cannellini), rinsed and drained
½ cup uncooked corkscrew-shaped pasta (rotini)
¼ cup grated Parmesan cheese (optional)

1. Heat the oil in a 6-quart saucepot. Add the zucchini, garlic and rosemary and cook until the zucchini is tender-crisp.

2. Stir the broth and tomatoes into the saucepot and heat to a boil. Reduce the heat to low. Cover and cook for 10 minutes.

3. Increase the heat to medium. Stir in the beans and pasta. Cook for 10 minutes or until the pasta is tender. Serve with the cheese, if desired.   *Makes 8 servings*

Prep Time: 10 minutes
Cook Time: 30 minutes

Tip "Ministra" is the Italian word for soup and minestrone means "big soup." Minestrone is always a thick, hearty soup, usually made with beans and pasta as well as an assortment of vegetables. With some crusty bread and a salad, minestrone makes a meal.

French Lentil Rice Soup

6 cups vegetable broth

1 cup dried lentils, rinsed and picked over

2 medium carrots, finely diced

1 small onion, finely chopped

2 stalks celery, finely diced

3 tablespoons uncooked rice

2 teaspoons minced garlic

1 teaspoon herbes de Provence

½ teaspoon salt

⅛ teaspoon ground black pepper

4 tablespoons whipping cream or sour cream

¼ cup chopped fresh parsley

Slow Cooker Directions

1. Stir together broth, lentils, carrots, onion, celery, rice, garlic, herbes de Provence, salt and pepper in slow cooker. Cover and cook on LOW 8 hours or on HIGH 4 to 5 hours.

2. Purée about 1½ cups of soup in food processor or blender until almost smooth. Stir back into remaining soup. Top each serving with spoonful of cream and sprinkle with parsley.

Makes 4 servings

Vegan Variation: Omit cream.

Small Plates

Spinach Artichoke Gratin

Nonstick cooking spray
2 cups (16 ounces) cottage cheese
2 eggs
4½ tablespoons grated Parmesan cheese, divided
1 tablespoon lemon juice
⅛ teaspoon black pepper
⅛ teaspoon ground nutmeg
2 packages (10 ounces each) frozen chopped spinach, thawed
⅓ cup thinly sliced green onions
1 package (10 ounces) frozen artichoke hearts, thawed and halved

1. Preheat oven to 375°F. Coat 1½-quart baking dish with nonstick cooking spray.

2. Process cottage cheese, eggs, 3 tablespoons Parmesan cheese, lemon juice, pepper and nutmeg in food processor until smooth.

3. Squeeze moisture from spinach. Combine spinach, cottage cheese mixture and green onions in large bowl. Spread half of mixture in baking dish.

4. Pat artichoke halves dry with paper towels. Place in single layer over spinach mixture. Sprinkle with remaining Parmesan cheese. Cover with remaining spinach mixture. Bake, covered, 25 minutes.

Makes 6 servings

Veggie-Stuffed Portobello Mushrooms

4 large portobello mushrooms (1¼ to 1½ pounds)
   Nonstick cooking spray
2 teaspoons olive oil or butter
1 cup chopped green or red bell pepper
⅓ cup sliced shallots or chopped onion
2 cloves garlic, minced
1 cup chopped zucchini or summer squash
½ teaspoon salt
¼ teaspoon black pepper
1 cup panko bread crumbs* or toasted fresh bread crumbs
1 cup (4 ounces) shredded sharp Cheddar or mozzarella cheese

Panko bread crumbs are light, crispy Japanese-style bread crumbs. They can be found in the Asian food aisle or with the bread crumbs in most supermarkets.

1. Preheat broiler. Line baking sheet with foil. Gently remove mushroom stems; chop and set aside. Scrape off and discard brown gills from mushroom caps with spoon. Place mushroom caps, top side up, on prepared baking sheet. Coat lightly with cooking spray. Broil 4 to 5 inches from heat 5 minutes or until tender.

2. Meanwhile, heat oil in large nonstick skillet over medium-high heat. Add bell pepper, shallots and garlic; cook and stir 5 minutes or until bell peppers begin to brown on edges. Stir in zucchini, reserved chopped mushroom stems, salt and black pepper; cook and stir 3 to 4 minutes or until vegetables are tender. Remove from heat; cool 5 minutes. Stir in bread crumbs and cheese.

3. Turn mushroom caps over. Mound vegetable mixture into caps. Broil 2 to 3 minutes or until golden brown and cheese is melted.   *Makes 4 servings*

Sizzling Rice Cakes with Mushrooms & Bell Peppers

¾ cup short grain rice*

1¾ cups water, divided

1 can (about 14 ounces) vegetable broth

1 tablespoon soy sauce

2 teaspoons sugar

2 teaspoons red wine vinegar

2 tablespoons cornstarch

3 tablespoons peanut oil, divided

1½ teaspoons finely chopped fresh ginger

2 cloves garlic, thinly sliced

1 red bell pepper, cut into short strips

1 green bell pepper, cut into short strips

8 ounces button mushrooms, quartered

4 ounces fresh shiitake or other exotic mushrooms, sliced

1 teaspoon sesame oil

Vegetable oil for frying

Short grain rice works best in this recipe because of its sticky texture when cooked. It may be labeled sweet or glutinous rice.

1. Rinse rice under cold running water to remove excess starch. Combine rice and 1½ cups water in medium saucepan. Bring to a boil over medium-high heat. Reduce heat to low; cover and simmer 15 to 20 minutes until liquid is absorbed. Let cool.

2. Combine broth, soy sauce, sugar and vinegar in medium bowl. Stir cornstarch into remaining ¼ cup water in small cup until smooth. Set aside.

3. Heat 1 tablespoon peanut oil in wok over medium-high heat. Add ginger and garlic; stir-fry 10 seconds. Add pepper strips; stir-fry 2 to 3 minutes or until crisp-tender. Remove and set aside.

4. Add remaining 2 tablespoons peanut oil to wok. Add mushrooms; stir-fry 2 to 3 minutes or until softened. Remove and set aside.

5. Add broth mixture to wok and bring to a boil. Stir cornstarch mixture; add to wok. Cook and stir until sauce boils and thickens slightly. Stir in sesame oil; return vegetables to wok. Remove from heat; cover and keep warm.

6. Shape rice into twelve 2-inch cakes. (Wet hands to make handling rice easier.)

7. Heat 2 to 3 inches vegetable oil in large skillet over medium-high heat until oil registers 375°F on deep-fry thermometer. Add 4 rice cakes; cook 2 to 3 minutes or until puffed and golden, turning once. Remove with slotted spatula to paper towels. Repeat with remaining rice cakes, reheating oil between batches.

8. Serve rice cakes with vegetable mixture.   *Makes 4 to 6 servings*

Stuffed Chayotes

2 large chayote squash*
2 tablespoons butter
½ cup chopped onion
1 clove garlic, minced
1 large tomato, peeled, seeded and chopped
2 tablespoons chopped fresh parsley
½ cup cooked corn
½ teaspoon salt
⅛ teaspoon black pepper
½ cup (2 ounces) shredded Cheddar cheese

For more information on chayote squash, see page 17 of the introduction.

1. Cut chayotes in half lengthwise; reserve pits. Place in microwavable dish, cut sides down; cook on HIGH 3½ minutes or until tender. When cool, remove pulp, leaving ½-inch shells; coarsely chop pulp and pits.

2. Preheat oven to 375°F. Melt butter in large skillet over medium heat. Brush inside of chayote shells with half of butter. Add onion and garlic to remaining butter in skillet; cook and stir 2 minutes or until onion is tender. Add tomato and parsley; simmer 5 minutes or until liquid has evaporated. Stir in corn, salt, pepper and chayote pulp.

3. Place chayote shells in greased shallow baking pan. Fill with vegetable mixture; top with cheese. Bake, uncovered, 15 minutes or until chayotes are hot and cheese is melted.

Makes 4 servings

Stuffed Summer Squash: Replace chayote squash with 8 large pattypan squash or 8 zucchini (about 6 inches long). Boil whole squash 8 to 10 minutes or until barely tender. After scooping out pulp, turn shells upside down on paper towels to drain before filling. Makes 8 servings.

Vegan Variation: Replace butter with oil and omit Cheddar cheese topping.

Greek Spanakopita

   Olive oil cooking spray
1 teaspoon olive oil
1 large onion, quartered and sliced
2 cloves garlic, minced
1 package (10 ounces) frozen chopped spinach, thawed and squeezed dry
½ cup feta cheese crumbles
5 sheets phyllo dough, thawed*
2 eggs, lightly beaten
¼ teaspoon nutmeg
¼ to ½ teaspoon black pepper
⅛ teaspoon salt

Thaw entire package of phyllo dough overnight in refrigerator.

1. Preheat oven to 375°F. Spray 8-inch square baking pan with cooking spray.

2. Heat oil in large skillet over medium heat. Add onion; cook and stir 7 to 8 minutes or until soft. Add garlic; cook and stir 30 seconds. Add spinach and cheese; cook and stir until spinach is heated through. Remove from heat.

3. Place one sheet of phyllo on counter with long side toward you. (Cover remaining sheets with damp towel until needed.) Spray right half of phyllo with cooking spray; fold left half over sprayed half. Place sheet in prepared pan. (Two edges will hang over sides of pan.) Spray top of sheet. Spray and fold two more sheets of phyllo the same way. Place sheets in pan at right angles so edges will hang over all four sides of pan. Spray each sheet after it is placed in pan.

4. Combine eggs, nutmeg, pepper and salt in small bowl. Stir into spinach mixture until blended. Spread filling over phyllo in pan. Spray and fold one sheet of phyllo as above; place on top of filling, tucking ends under filling. Bring all overhanging edges of phyllo over top sheet; spray lightly. Spray and fold last sheet as above; place over top sheet, tucking ends under. Spray lightly. Bake 25 to 27 minutes or until top is barely browned. Cool 10 to 15 minutes before serving.   *Makes 4 servings*

Veggie Tostadas

1 tablespoon olive oil

1 cup chopped onion

1 cup chopped celery

2 cloves garlic, chopped

1 can (about 15 ounces) red kidney beans, rinsed and drained

1 can (about 15 ounces) Great Northern beans, rinsed and drained

1 can (about 14 ounces) salsa-style diced tomatoes

2 teaspoons chili powder

1 teaspoon ground cumin

6 (6-inch) corn tortillas

   Toppings: Chopped fresh cilantro, shredded lettuce, chopped seeded fresh tomatoes, shredded Cheddar cheese and sour cream (optional)

1. Heat oil in large skillet over medium heat. Add onion, celery and garlic. Cook and stir 8 minutes or until softened. Stir in beans, tomatoes, chili powder and cumin. Reduce heat to medium-low. Simmer 30 minutes, stirring occasionally, until thickened.

2. Meanwhile, preheat oven to 400°F. Place tortillas in single layer directly on oven rack. Bake 10 to 12 minutes or until crisp. Place one tortilla on each plate. Spoon bean mixture evenly over each tortilla. Top with cilantro, lettuce, tomatoes, Cheddar cheese and sour cream, if desired.   *Makes 6 servings*

Vegan Variation: Replace cheese and sour cream topping with dairy-free variations, sliced avocados or guacamole.

Artichokes with Lemon-Tarragon Butter

6 cups water

2¼ teaspoons salt, divided

2 whole artichokes, stems cut off and leaf tips trimmed

¼ cup (½ stick) unsalted butter

¼ teaspoon grated lemon peel

2 tablespoons lemon juice

¼ teaspoon dried tarragon

1. Bring water and 2 teaspoons salt to a boil in large saucepan over high heat. Add artichokes; return to a boil. Reduce heat to medium-low; cover and simmer 35 to 45 minutes or until leaves detach easily (cooking time will depend on artichoke size).

2. Turn artichokes upside down on paper towels to drain well. When cool enough to handle, cut artichokes in half; remove fuzzy inedible choke at base of leaves.

3. Combine butter, lemon peel and juice, tarragon and remaining ¼ teaspoon salt in small saucepan; heat until butter melts. Serve in small bowls for dipping.

Makes 2 servings

Tip When cooking artichokes it's important to use a saucepan made of stainless steel or other nonreactive material. An unlined aluminum or cast iron pan can discolor artichokes and give them a metallic taste. Adding some lemon juice or vinegar to the cooking water will help keep the artichokes from darkening and add flavor. Cooked artichokes can be wrapped in plastic and refrigerated for up to four days.

Tamales

1 package dried corn husks

1 can (about 15 ounces) yellow corn, drained, liquid reserved

1 to 1⅜ cups cornmeal

2 tablespoons softened butter

1 teaspoon salt

4 ounces quesadilla cheese or mozzarella cheese

1 can (about 7 ounces) pickled jalapeños

Salsa, pico de gallo or guacamole

1. Soak corn husks in warm water 1 hour or until softened.

2. Place corn and 2 tablespoons reserved corn liquid in food processor. Pulse until paste forms. Add 1 cup cornmeal, butter and salt. Pulse 1 minute or until dough forms. Add more cornmeal gradually until dough is soft and moist, but not sticky. Transfer dough to work surface and keep covered to prevent drying out.

3. Drain corn husks and pat dry. Cut cheese into 4-inch-long sticks about ½-inch in diameter. Cut jalapeños into strips. Tear narrow strips of corn husk to use as ties for tamales.*

4. Place corn husk on work surface. Place 2 tablespoons of cornmeal mixture on husk about one third of the way from top. Pat dough into 4-inch-long by 2-inch wide rectangle. Arrange 1 strip of cheese and 1 strip of jalapeño in center of dough.

5. Lift sides of husk to enclose filling in dough and wrap gently around tamale. Fold bottom of husk over tamale; tie closed with strip of husk. Top of tamale may be left open or tied shut. Transfer tamales to steamer basket.

6. Bring large saucepan half filled with water to a boil. Place steamer over water. (Tamales should not touch water.) Cover; steam 45 minutes to 1 hour or until tamale dough no longer sticks to corn husk, adding water as needed.

7. Serve tamales in husks. Unwrap just before eating and top with salsa. Tamales may also be refrigerated or frozen in husks and reheated in steamer or microwave.

Makes 8 tamales

You can also secure tamales with kitchen twine, if desired.

Fried Tofu with Sesame Dipping Sauce

3 tablespoons soy sauce or tamari

2 tablespoons unseasoned rice wine vinegar

2 teaspoons sugar

1 teaspoon sesame seeds, toasted*

1 teaspoon dark sesame oil

⅛ teaspoon red pepper flakes

1 package (about 14 ounces) extra firm tofu

2 tablespoons all-purpose flour

1 egg

¾ cup panko bread crumbs

4 tablespoons vegetable oil

To toast sesame seeds, spread seeds in small skillet. Shake skillet over medium-low heat about 3 minutes or until seeds begin to pop and turn golden.

1. For dipping sauce, combine soy sauce, vinegar, sugar, sesame seeds, sesame oil and red pepper flakes in small bowl. Set aside.

2. Drain tofu on paper towels to remove excess water. Cut crosswise into four slices; cut each slice diagonally into triangles. Place flour in shallow dish. Beat egg in shallow bowl. Place panko in another shallow bowl.

3. Dip each piece of tofu in flour to lightly coat all sides; dip in egg, turning to coat. Drain; roll in panko to coat lightly.

4. Heat 2 tablespoons vegetable oil in large nonstick skillet over high heat. Reduce heat to medium; add half of tofu in single layer. Cook 1 to 2 minutes per side or until golden brown. Repeat with remaining tofu. Serve with dipping sauce.

Makes 4 servings

Swiss Chard Flavor Packet

   2 to 2½ pounds Swiss chard
   1 cup diced onion
   1 cup diced red bell pepper
   ½ cup diced carrot
   ½ cup chopped cilantro or parsley
   3 tablespoons fresh lime juice
   1 tablespoon minced garlic
   1 tablespoon olive oil
   ½ teaspoon salt
   ¼ teaspoon black pepper

1. Preheat oven to 350°F. Separate chard leaves from stalks. Cut stalks into ½-inch dice. Roll chard leaves into bundles and chop. Toss chard, onion, bell pepper, carrot, cilantro, lime juice, garlic, olive oil, salt and black pepper in large bowl.

2. Tear 20×16-inch sheet of heavy-duty foil. Place on baking sheet and spray with nonstick cooking spray. Place chard mixture on half of foil; fold over and crimp edges to make a packet. Bake 25 to 35 minutes or until chard is tender.   *Makes 4 servings*

Tip Swiss chard is a member of the beet family and comes in a variety of colors. Regular chard has crinkly green leaves and silvery stalks. Rhubarb chard has red stalks and dark green leaves. The chard in the photo is called rainbow chard and features red, white and golden stems. In addition to being colorful, chard is very nutritious. It's high in vitamins A, C, E, K and is a good source of fiber.

Socca (Niçoise Chickpea Pancake)

1 cup chickpea flour*
¾ teaspoon salt
½ teaspoon ground pepper
1 cup water
5 tablespoons olive oil, divided
1½ teaspoons minced fresh basil *or* ½ teaspoon dried basil
1 teaspoon minced fresh rosemary *or* ¼ teaspoon dried rosemary
¼ teaspoon dried thyme

Chickpea flour is also called garbanzo flour. It is found in the specialty food section of most supermarkets.

1. Sift chickpea flour into medium bowl. Stir in salt and pepper. Gradually whisk in water to create a smooth batter. Stir in 2 tablespoons olive oil. Allow batter to rest at least 30 minutes.

2. Preheat oven to 450°F about 10 minutes before ready to bake socca. Place 9- or 10-inch cast iron skillet in oven to heat.

3. Add basil, rosemary and thyme to batter; whisk until smooth. Carefully remove skillet from oven using oven mitts. Add 2 tablespoons olive oil to skillet; swirl to coat evenly. Immediately pour in batter.

4. Bake socca 12 to 15 minutes or until edge begins to pull away and center is firm. Remove skillet; turn oven to broil.

5. Brush socca with remaining tablespoon oil and broil 2 to 4 minutes until dark brown in spots. Cut into wedges and serve warm.   *Makes 6 servings*

Tip Socca, pancakes made of chickpea flour, are commonly served in paper cones as a savory street food in the south of France, especially around Nice. Chickpea flour can also be used to make a thinner batter and cooked in a skillet to make a softer crêpe. Just increase the amount of water in the recipe by about ¼ cup.

Oven-Roasted Root Vegetables

Vegetable cooking spray

3 medium red potatoes (about 1 pound), cut into 1-inch pieces

2 cups fresh or frozen whole baby carrots

1 pound celery root (celeriac), peeled and cut into 1-inch pieces (about 2 cups)

1 rutabaga (about 3 pounds), peeled and cut into 1-inch pieces (about 6 cups)

2 medium red onions, cut into 8 wedges each

2 medium parsnips, peeled and cut into 1-inch pieces (about 1½ cups)

5 cloves garlic, cut into thin slices

1 tablespoon chopped fresh rosemary leaves or fresh thyme leaves

1 tablespoon olive oil

1 cup SWANSON® Vegetable Broth (Regular or Certified Organic)

1. Heat the oven to 425°F. Spray a 17×11-inch roasting pan or shallow baking sheet with the cooking spray.

2. Stir the potatoes, carrots, celery root, rutabaga, onions, parsnips, garlic, rosemary and oil in the prepared pan. Roast the vegetables for 30 minutes. Pour the broth over the vegetables and stir.

3. Roast for 20 minutes or until the vegetables are fork-tender.   *Makes 8 servings*

Prep Time: 35 minutes
Cook Time: 50 minutes
Total Time: 1 hour 25 minutes

Mushroom and Arugula Quiche

    1 tablespoon olive oil
  ½ cup chopped onion
    2 cloves garlic, minced
1½ cups sliced mushrooms (5 to 6 ounces)
    1 package (5 ounces) DOLE® Baby Arugula with Baby Spinach Blend
    1 cup (4 ounces) shredded Swiss cheese
    1 (9-inch) frozen deep-dish pie shell, thawed
  ¼ cup grated Parmesan cheese, divided
    4 eggs, well beaten
  ½ cup half-and-half
  ¼ teaspoon salt
    Pinch ground black pepper
    Pinch ground nutmeg

• Preheat oven to 375°F.

• Heat oil in large nonstick skillet over medium-high heat. Add onion and garlic; cook, stirring often, until tender, 3 to 4 minutes. Add mushrooms; cook, stirring occasionally, until excess moisture has evaporated and mushrooms start to brown, 4 to 5 minutes. Add the salad blend and cook, stirring until wilted and almost dry, 3 to 4 minutes. Remove from heat; cool slightly.

• Mix together cooled vegetables and Swiss cheese. Sprinkle half of Parmesan cheese on bottom of pie shell. Top with vegetable mixture.

• Stir together eggs, half-and-half, salt and spices; pour into the pie shell. Sprinkle with remaining Parmesan cheese. Bake 30 minutes or until knife inserted near center comes out clean.

Makes 4 to 6 servings

Prep Time: 15 minutes
Bake Time: 30 minutes

Falafel with Garlic Tahini Sauce

1 cup dried chickpeas, sorted and rinsed
 Garlic Tahini Sauce (page 79)
1 small onion
½ cup chopped fresh parsley
 2 cloves garlic
 2 teaspoons ground cumin
 1 teaspoon ground coriander
¼ cup fresh lemon juice
½ teaspoon salt
½ teaspoon ground red pepper
 Vegetable oil
 Pita bread, lettuce, tomatoes and chopped cucumbers

1. Soak chickpeas overnight in large bowl with water to cover by at least 3 inches. (Chickpeas will triple in volume.) Prepare Garlic Tahini Sauce; refrigerate until ready to serve.

2. Drain chickpeas well and transfer to food processor. Add all remaining ingredients except oil. Pulse until mixture is smooth, scraping side of bowl frequently. If mixture is too dry, add 1 to 2 tablespoons water.

3. Scoop out heaping tablespoons of mixture. Shape into 1½-inch balls with dampened hands. Place on baking sheet lined with waxed paper.

4. Pour oil into deep heavy saucepan to depth of 2 inches. Heat over medium-high heat to 350°F. Fry falafel in batches 3 to 5 minutes or until golden brown. Remove with slotted spoon and drain on paper towels.

5. Serve with Garlic Tahini Sauce, pita bread, lettuce, tomatoes and cucumbers.

Makes 8 servings

Garlic Tahini Sauce

½ **cup plain yogurt**

¼ **cup tahini***

 3 **tablespoons water**

 2 **tablespoons fresh lemon juice**

 1 **clove garlic, minced**

½ **teaspoon cumin**

  Salt and black pepper to taste

*Tahini is a thick paste made from ground sesame seeds and is used in Middle Eastern cooking. It is available in many large supermarkets.

Whisk all ingredients in small bowl until well blended. Cover; refrigerate 1 hour.

Makes about 1 cup

Spinach Soufflé

  1 pound fresh spinach leaves
¼ cup (½ stick) butter
  1 tablespoon finely chopped shallot
¼ cup all-purpose flour
¼ teaspoon salt
¼ teaspoon ground nutmeg
⅛ teaspoon ground white pepper
1½ cups milk, at room temperature
  6 eggs, separated
½ cup freshly grated Parmesan cheese
    Pinch cream of tartar (optional)

1. Preheat oven to 375°F. Grease 2-quart soufflé dish or deep casserole.

2. Bring large saucepan of salted water to a boil over high heat. Add spinach; cook 1 to 2 minutes or until wilted. Drain and immediately plunge into cold water to stop cooking. When cool enough to handle, squeeze out excess moisture. Finely chop spinach (makes about 1 cup).

3. Melt butter in large saucepan over medium heat. Add shallot; cook and stir 2 to 3 minutes. Stir in flour, salt, nutmeg and pepper. Gradually stir in milk. Cook and stir until mixture comes to a boil and thickens. Let cool slightly.

4. Stir egg yolks into saucepan until well blended. Add spinach and cheese; mix well.

5. Meanwhile, place egg whites in clean large bowl with cream of tartar. Beat with electric mixer at high speed until egg whites form stiff peaks.

6. Gently fold egg whites into spinach mixture until almost combined. (Some white streaks should remain.) Transfer mixture to prepared dish.

7. Bake 30 to 40 minutes or until puffed and golden and wooden skewer inserted into center comes out moist but clean. Serve immediately. *Makes 4 servings*

Asian Influence

Teriyaki Tempeh with Pineapple

1 package (8 ounces) unseasoned soy tempeh*
1 cup pineapple teriyaki sauce, plus additional as needed
4 fresh pineapple rings
1 cup uncooked rice
½ cup julienned carrots
½ cup snow peas
½ cup matchstick-size red bell pepper strips

For more information on tempeh, see page 26 of the introduction.

1. Place 1 cup water in large deep skillet; heat over high heat. Halve tempeh crosswise; add to skillet. Bring to a boil; reduce heat and boil gently 10 minutes. Drain water; add 1 cup teriyaki sauce to tempeh in skillet. Boil gently 10 minutes, turning tempeh occasionally. Drain and reserve teriyaki sauce; add additional sauce to make ½ cup.

2. Meanwhile, cook rice according to package directions. Heat reserved teriyaki sauce in wok or large nonstick skillet over medium-high heat. Add carrots, snow peas and bell pepper; cook and stir 4 to 6 minutes or until crisp-tender. Add rice; stir to combine. Add additional teriyaki sauce, if desired.

3. Preheat grill to medium-high. Grill tempeh and pineapple rings 5 minutes per side. Cut tempeh in half; serve with rice and pineapple. *Makes 4 servings*

Island Tempeh Sandwich: Omit rice and vegetables. Serve tempeh and pineapple on a soft roll with arugula, additional teriyaki sauce and desired condiments.

Vegetarian Summer Rolls

½ cup soy sauce, divided
2 tablespoons lime juice
1 tablespoon sugar
2 cloves garlic, crushed
1 teaspoon rice vinegar
1 package (14 ounces) firm tofu, drained and pressed*
2 medium portobello mushrooms, cut into thin strips
1 teaspoon dark sesame oil
1 tablespoon vegetable oil
1 tablespoon sesame seeds
3½ ounces thin rice noodles (rice vermicelli)
12 rice paper wrappers**
1 bunch fresh mint
½ cup shredded carrots
1 yellow bell pepper, cut into thin strips

To press tofu, cut it in half horizontally and place it between layers of paper towels. Place a cutting board and heavy cans on top for 15 to 30 minutes.

**Rice paper is a thin, edible wrapper used in Southeast Asian cooking. See page 24 of the introduction.*

1. For dipping sauce, combine ¼ cup soy sauce, lime juice, sugar, garlic and vinegar in small bowl. Stir until sugar is dissolved. Set aside.

2. Cut tofu into narrow strips about ¼ inch thick. Place in medium bowl with mushrooms. Add remaining ¼ cup soy sauce and sesame oil; toss gently. Heat vegetable oil in large skillet over medium heat. Brown tofu and mushrooms; sprinkle with sesame seeds.

3. Place rice noodles in medium bowl; cover with hot water. Soak 15 to 30 minutes or until softened. Drain; cut into 3-inch lengths.

4. Soften one rice paper wrapper in bowl of warm water 20 to 30 seconds. Place on flat surface lined with dish towel. Arrange mint leaves in center of wrapper. Top with tofu, mushrooms, carrots, noodles and bell pepper.

5. Fold bottom of wrapper up over filling; fold in each side and roll up. Repeat with remaining wrappers. Wrap finished rolls individually in plastic wrap or cover with damp towel to prevent drying out. Serve with dipping sauce.

Makes 12 summer rolls

Thai Seitan Stir-Fry

1 package (8 ounces) seitan,* drained and thinly sliced

1 jalapeño pepper, halved and seeded

3 cloves garlic

1 piece peeled fresh ginger (about 1 inch)

⅓ cup soy sauce

¼ cup packed brown sugar

¼ cup lime juice (2 limes)

½ teaspoon red pepper flakes

¼ teaspoon salt

3 tablespoons vegetable oil

1 medium onion, chopped (about 2 cups)

2 red bell peppers, quartered and thinly sliced (about 2 cups)

2 cups fresh broccoli florets

¼ cup shredded fresh basil

3 green onions, sliced diagonally

4 cups lightly packed baby spinach

3 cups hot cooked rice

¼ cup salted peanuts, chopped

Seitan is a meat substitute made from wheat gluten. See page 27 of the introduction for more information.

1. Place seitan slices in medium bowl. Combine jalapeño, garlic and ginger in food processor; process until finely chopped. Add soy sauce, brown sugar, lime juice, red pepper flakes and salt; process until blended. Pour mixture over seitan; toss to coat. Marinate at least 20 minutes at room temperature.

2. Heat oil in wok or large skillet over high heat. Add onion, bell peppers and broccoli; stir-fry 3 to 5 minutes. Add seitan with marinade and green onions. Bring to a boil; stir-fry 3 minutes or until vegetables are crisp-tender and seitan is hot. Add spinach in batches, stirring until wilted.

3. Stir in basil just before serving. Serve over rice; sprinkle with peanuts.

Makes 4 to 6 servings

Sesame Peanut Spaghetti Squash

1 spaghetti squash (about 3 pounds)

⅓ cup sesame seeds

⅓ cup vegetable broth

2 tablespoons soy sauce

1 tablespoon sugar

2 teaspoons dark sesame oil

1 teaspoon cornstarch

1 teaspoon red pepper flakes

1 tablespoon vegetable oil

2 medium carrots, julienned

1 large red bell pepper, thinly sliced

¼ pound fresh snow peas, cut in half

½ cup chopped unsalted peanuts

⅓ cup minced fresh cilantro

1. Preheat oven to 350°F. Spray 13×9-inch baking dish with nonstick cooking spray. Cut squash in half lengthwise. Remove and discard seeds. Place squash, cut side down, in prepared dish. Bake 45 minutes to 1 hour or until tender.

2. Using oven mitts to hold squash, remove spaghetti-like strands with fork. Place strands in large bowl; cover and keep warm.

3. Heat wok or large skillet over medium-high. Add sesame seeds; cook and stir 45 seconds or until golden brown. Transfer to blender; add broth, soy sauce, sugar, sesame oil, cornstarch and red pepper flakes. Process until mixture is coarsely puréed.

4. Heat oil in wok or large skillet over medium-high heat 1 minute. Add carrots; stir-fry 1 minute. Add bell pepper; stir-fry 2 minutes or until vegetables are crisp-tender. Add snow peas; stir-fry 1 minute. Stir sesame seed mixture; add to wok. Cook and stir 1 minute or until sauce is thickened.

5. Serve sauce over spaghetti squash. Top with peanuts and cilantro.

Makes 4 servings

Soba Stir-Fry

8 ounces uncooked soba (buckwheat) noodles
1 tablespoon olive oil
2 cups sliced shiitake mushrooms
1 medium red bell pepper, cut into thin strips
2 whole dried red chiles *or* ¼ teaspoon red pepper flakes
1 clove garlic, minced
2 cups shredded napa cabbage
½ cup vegetable broth
2 tablespoons tamari or soy sauce
1 tablespoon rice wine or dry sherry
2 teaspoons cornstarch
1 package (14 ounces) firm tofu, drained and cut into 1-inch cubes
2 green onions, thinly sliced

1. Cook noodles according to package directions. Drain and set aside.

2. Heat oil in large wok or skillet over medium heat. Add mushrooms, bell pepper, dried chiles and garlic. Cook and stir 3 minutes or until mushrooms are tender. Add cabbage. Cover; cook 2 minutes or until cabbage is wilted.

3. Combine broth, tamari, rice wine and cornstarch in small bowl. Stir sauce into vegetable mixture. Cook and stir 2 minutes or until sauce is thickened.

4. Stir in tofu and noodles; toss gently until heated through. Sprinkle with green onions. Serve immediately.

Makes 4 servings

Beer Batter Tempura

1½ cups all-purpose flour
1½ cups cold Japanese beer
1 teaspoon salt
Dipping Sauce (recipe follows)
Vegetable oil for frying
½ pound green beans or asparagus tips
1 large sweet potato, peeled and cut into ¼-inch slices
1 medium eggplant, cut into ¼-inch slices

1. Combine flour, beer and salt in medium bowl just until mixed. *Do not overmix.* Batter should be thin and lumpy. Set aside 15 minutes. Meanwhile, prepare Dipping Sauce.

2. Heat 1 inch of oil in large saucepan to 375°F; adjust heat to maintain temperature.

3. Dip 10 to 12 green beans in batter; add to hot oil. Fry until light golden brown. Remove to wire racks or paper towels to drain; keep warm. Repeat with remaining vegetables, working with only one vegetable at a time and being careful not to crowd vegetables. Serve with Dipping Sauce. *Makes 4 servings*

Dipping Sauce

½ cup soy sauce
2 tablespoons rice wine
1 tablespoon sugar
½ teaspoon white vinegar
2 teaspoons minced fresh ginger
1 clove garlic, minced
2 green onions, thinly sliced

Combine soy sauce, rice wine, sugar and vinegar in small saucepan. Cook and stir over medium heat 3 minutes or until sugar dissolves. Add ginger and garlic; cook 2 minutes. Add green onions; remove from heat. *Make 4 servings*

Ma Po Tofu

1 package (14 ounces) firm tofu, drained and pressed*

2 tablespoons soy sauce

2 teaspoons minced fresh ginger

1 cup vegetable broth, divided

2 tablespoons black bean sauce

1 tablespoon sweet chili sauce

1 tablespoon cornstarch

2 tablespoons vegetable oil

1 green bell pepper, cut into bite-size pieces

2 cloves garlic, minced

1½ cups broccoli florets

¼ cup chopped fresh cilantro (optional)

Hot cooked rice

To press tofu, cut it in half horizontally and place it between layers of paper towels. Place a cutting board and heavy cans on top for 15 to 30 minutes.

1. Cut tofu into ¾-inch squares or triangles. Place in shallow dish; sprinkle with soy sauce and ginger.

2. Stir together ¼ cup broth, black bean sauce, chili sauce and cornstarch in small bowl; set aside.

3. Heat oil in wok or large skillet over high heat. Add bell pepper and garlic; cook and stir 2 minutes. Add remaining ¾ cup broth and broccoli; bring to a boil. Reduce heat; cover and simmer 3 minutes or until broccoli is crisp-tender.

4. Stir sauce mixture and add to wok. Cook and stir 1 minute or until sauce boils and thickens. Stir in tofu and simmer, uncovered, until heated through. Sprinkle with cilantro. Serve with rice.   *Makes 4 servings*

Buddha's Delight

1 package (1 ounce) dried shiitake mushrooms

1 package (14 ounces) firm tofu, drained and pressed*

1 tablespoon peanut or vegetable oil

2 cups diagonally cut 1-inch asparagus pieces

1 medium onion, cut into thin wedges

2 cloves garlic, minced

½ cup vegetable broth

3 tablespoons hoisin sauce

¼ cup coarsely chopped fresh cilantro or thinly sliced green onions

To press tofu, cut it in half horizontally and place it between layers of paper towels. Place a cutting board and heavy cans on top for 15 to 30 minutes.

1. Place mushrooms in small bowl; cover with warm water. Soak 20 minutes to soften. Drain in fine strainer over measuring cup, squeezing out excess liquid; reserve liquid. Discard mushroom stems; slice caps. Cut tofu into ¾-inch cubes.

2. Heat oil in wok or large skillet over medium-high heat. Add asparagus, onion wedges and garlic; stir-fry 4 minutes.

3. Add mushrooms, ¼ cup reserved mushroom liquid, broth and hoisin sauce. Reduce heat to medium-low. Simmer, uncovered, 2 to 3 minute or until asparagus is crisp-tender.

4. Stir in tofu; heat through, stirring occasionally. Ladle into shallow bowls. Sprinkle with cilantro. *Makes 2 servings*

Mu Shu Vegetables

Peanut Sauce (page 99)
3 tablespoons soy sauce
1½ tablespoons minced fresh ginger
2 tablespoons dry sherry
2 teaspoons cornstarch
3 cloves garlic, minced
1½ teaspoons sesame oil
1 tablespoon peanut oil
3 leeks, cut into 2-inch slivers
3 carrots, julienned
1 cup thinly sliced fresh shiitake mushrooms
1 small head Napa or Savoy cabbage, shredded (about 4 cups)
2 cups mung bean sprouts, rinsed and drained
8 ounces firm tofu, drained and cut into strips
12 (8-inch) flour tortillas, warmed*
¾ cup finely chopped roasted peanuts

Tortillas can be softened and warmed in microwave oven just before using. Stack tortillas and wrap in plastic wrap. Microwave on HIGH 30 seconds to 1 minute, turning once.

1. Prepare Peanut Sauce; set aside. Mix soy sauce, ginger, sherry, cornstarch, garlic and sesame oil in small bowl until smooth; set aside.

2. Heat peanut oil in wok or large skillet over medium-high heat. Add leeks, carrots and mushrooms; stir-fry 2 minutes. Add cabbage; stir-fry 3 minutes or until softened. Add bean sprouts and tofu; stir-fry 1 minute or until hot. Stir soy sauce mixture; add to wok. Cook and stir 1 minute or until sauce is thickened.

3. Spread each tortilla with about 1 teaspoon Peanut Sauce. Spoon ½ cup vegetable mixture onto bottom half of each tortilla; sprinkle with 1 tablespoon peanuts.

4. Fold bottom edge of tortilla over filling; fold in side edges. Roll up to enclose filling. Serve with remaining Peanut Sauce. *Makes 6 servings*

Peanut Sauce

3 tablespoons sugar

3 tablespoons water

3 tablespoons dry sherry

3 tablespoons soy sauce

2 teaspoons white wine vinegar

⅓ cup creamy peanut butter

Combine sugar, water, sherry, soy sauce and vinegar in small saucepan. Bring to a boil over medium-high heat, stirring constantly. Boil 1 minute or until sugar dissolves. Stir in peanut butter until smooth; cool to room temperature.   *Makes ⅔ cup*

Thai Veggie Curry

2 tablespoons vegetable oil

1 onion, quartered and thinly sliced

1 tablespoon Thai red curry paste (or to taste)

1 can (about 13 ounces) unsweetened coconut milk

2 red or yellow bell peppers, cut into strips

1½ cups cauliflower and/or broccoli florets

1 cup snow peas

1 package (14 ounces) firm tofu, pressed* and cubed

Salt and pepper

¼ cup slivered fresh basil

Hot cooked jasmine rice

To press tofu, cut it in half horizontally and place it between layers of paper towels. Place a cutting board and heavy cans on top for 15 to 30 minutes.

1. Heat oil in large skillet or wok over medium-high heat. Add onion; cook and stir 2 minutes or until softened. Add curry paste; cook and stir to coat onion. Add coconut milk; bring to a boil, stirring to dissolve curry paste.

2. Add bell peppers and cauliflower; simmer over medium heat 4 to 5 minutes or until crisp-tender. Stir in snow peas; simmer 2 minutes. Gently stir in tofu; cook until heated through.

3. Sprinkle with basil; serve with rice.   *Makes 4 to 6 servings*

 *Tip* Coconut milk is not, as you might expect, the liquid inside a coconut. That is coconut water, a refreshing drink. To make coconut milk, shredded fresh coconut meat is combined with hot water. This mixture is then squeezed to extract the rich white "milk." Fresh and canned coconut milk separate into two layers. The top layer is the coconut cream; the thinner bottom layer is the milk. Shake the can of coconut milk to combine them before opening it.

Vegetable Lo Mein

8 ounces uncooked Chinese thin wheat noodles (mein) or thin spaghetti

2 egg whites

1 egg

1 green onion, thinly sliced

Nonstick cooking spray

1 tablespoon dark sesame oil

4 ounces shiitake mushrooms, stemmed and sliced *or* 1 package (4 ounces) sliced exotic mushrooms

2 cups thinly sliced bok choy

1 small red or yellow bell pepper, cut into strips

½ cup vegetable broth

¼ cup teriyaki sauce

Chopped peanuts (optional)

Chopped cilantro (optional)

1. Cook noodles according to package directions. Drain and set aside.

2. Meanwhile, beat egg whites and egg until frothy. Stir in green onion. Spray large nonstick skillet with nonstick cooking spray; heat over medium heat. Add egg mixture; cook without stirring 2 to 3 minutes or until set on bottom. Carefully flip egg pancake; cook 1 minute or until set on bottom. Transfer to cutting board; set aside.

3. Heat oil in same skillet over medium-high heat. Add mushrooms, bok choy and bell pepper; cook 4 to 5 minutes or until vegetables are tender. Add broth and teriyaki sauce; simmer 2 minutes.

4. Add vegetables to noodles; toss well. Cut egg pancake into strips. Gently toss strips with noodle mixture. Transfer to shallow serving bowls; sprinkle with peanuts and cilantro, if desired.   *Makes 4 servings*

Mongolian Vegetables

1 package (14 ounces) firm tofu, drained and pressed*

4 tablespoons soy sauce, divided

1 tablespoon dark sesame oil

1 large head bok choy (about 1½ pounds)

2 teaspoons sesame seeds

2 teaspoons cornstarch

1 tablespoon peanut or vegetable oil

1 red or yellow bell pepper, cut into short thin strips

2 cloves garlic, minced

4 green onions, cut into ½-inch pieces

*To press tofu, cut it in half horizontally and place it between layers of paper towels. Place a cutting board and heavy cans on top for 15 to 30 minutes.

1. Cut tofu into ¾-inch squares. Place in shallow dish. Combine 2 tablespoons soy sauce and sesame oil in small bowl; drizzle over tofu. Let stand while preparing vegetables.

2. Cut stems from bok choy leaves; slice stems into ½-inch pieces. Cut leaves crosswise into ½-inch slices. Spread sesame seeds in small skillet. Shake skillet over medium-low heat 3 minutes or until seeds begin to pop and turn golden.

3. Blend remaining 2 tablespoons soy sauce into cornstarch in small bowl until smooth.

4. Heat peanut oil in wok or large skillet over medium-high heat. Add bok choy stems, bell pepper and garlic; stir-fry 5 minutes. Add bok choy leaves and green onions; stir-fry 2 minutes.

5. Stir cornstarch mixture and add to wok along with tofu mixture. Stir-fry 30 seconds or until sauce boils and thickens. Sprinkle with sesame seeds.　　*Makes 2 servings*

Vegetarian Sushi

1¼ cups Japanese short grain sushi rice*
1½ cups water
1 teaspoon dark sesame oil
4 medium shiitake mushrooms, thinly sliced
½ red bell pepper
½ unpeeled seedless cucumber
4 thin asparagus spears
2½ tablespoons seasoned rice vinegar
3 sheets nori (from .6 ounce package)
Prepared wasabi
Pickled ginger, soy sauce and additional prepared wasabi

*If you can't find white rice labeled "sushi rice," use any short grain rice.

1. Rinse rice in several changes of water to remove excess starch; drain. Combine rice and 1½ cups water in medium saucepan and bring to a boil. Reduce heat to very low. Cook, covered, 15 to 20 minutes until rice is tender and liquid is absorbed. Let stand 10 minutes, covered.

2. Meanwhile, prepare fillings. Heat small nonstick skillet over medium heat; add sesame oil. Cook and stir mushrooms 2 to 3 minutes or until tender. Slice bell pepper into very thin, long pieces. Cut cucumber into thin, long slivers. Wrap damp asparagus loosely in plastic wrap and microwave 1 minute to blanch.

3. Spoon warm rice into shallow nonmetallic bowl. Sprinkle vinegar over rice and fold in gently with wooden spoon. Cut sheet of nori in half lengthwise, parallel to lines marked on rough side. Place lengthwise, shiny side down, on bamboo rolling mat about 3 slats from edge nearest to you.

4. Prepare small bowl with water and splash of vinegar to rinse fingers and prevent rice from sticking while working. Spread about ½ cup rice over nori, leaving ½-inch border at top edge. Spread pinch of wasabi across center of rice. Arrange strips of two different fillings over wasabi. Do not overfill.

5. Pick up edge of mat nearest you. Roll mat forward, wrapping rice around fillings and pressing gently to form log. Once roll is formed, press gently to seal; place completed roll on cutting board, seam side down. Repeat with remaining nori and fillings.

6. Slice each roll into 6 pieces with sharp knife. Wipe knife with damp cloth between cuts. Arrange sushi on serving plates with pickled ginger, soy sauce and additional wasabi for dipping.   *Makes 6 sushi rolls (36 pieces)*

Rice Noodles with Broccoli & Tofu

1 package (14 ounces) firm tofu, drained and pressed*
1 package (8 to 10 ounces) wide rice noodles
2 tablespoons peanut oil
3 medium shallots, sliced
6 cloves garlic, minced
1 jalapeño pepper, minced
2 teaspoons minced fresh ginger
3 cups broccoli florets
3 tablespoons regular soy sauce
1 tablespoon sweet soy sauce** (or substitute regular)
1 to 2 tablespoons vegetarian fish sauce or additional sweet soy sauce
    Fresh basil leaves (optional)

To press tofu, cut it in half horizontally and place it between layers of paper towels. Place a cutting board and heavy cans on top for 15 to 30 minutes.

**Sweet soy sauce is thicker and darker than regular soy sauce and has a richer flavor.*

1. Place rice noodles in large bowl; cover with hot water. Soak 30 minutes or until soft.

2. Cut tofu into bite-size squares and blot dry. Heat oil in large skillet or wok over medium-high heat. Add tofu to skillet; stir-fry about 5 minutes or until tofu is lightly browned on all sides. Remove from skillet.

3. Add shallots, garlic, jalapeño pepper and ginger to skillet. Stir-fry 2 to 3 minutes. Add broccoli; stir-fry 1 minute. Cover and cook 3 minutes or until broccoli is crisp-tender.

4. Drain noodles; add to skillet and stir to combine. Return tofu to skillet; add soy sauces and fish sauce. Stir-fry about 8 minutes or until noodles are coated and flavors are blended. Garnish with basil.

Makes 4 to 6 servings

Pasta & Noodles

Vegan Pesto

1 pound uncooked whole wheat fettuccine

1 cup packed fresh basil leaves

½ cup pine nuts, toasted*

2 cloves garlic

½ teaspoon salt

¼ teaspoon black pepper

¼ cup plus 1 tablespoon olive oil

Place pine nuts in small saucepan. Heat over low heat 2 minutes or until light brown and fragrant, shaking occasionally.

1. Cook pasta according to package directions. Drain; set aside and keep warm.

2. Meanwhile, place basil, pine nuts, garlic, salt and pepper in food processor; drizzle with 1 tablespoon olive oil. Process about 10 seconds or until coarsely chopped. Scrape down side of bowl. With motor running, drizzle in remaining ¼ cup olive oil. Process about 30 seconds or until almost smooth. Toss with hot cooked pasta.

Makes 4 servings

Note: Pesto can be made one week in advance. Transfer to covered container and store in refrigerator. Makes ½ cup pesto.

Lasagna Florentine with Provolone & Portobello Mushrooms

2 cups (15 ounces) SARGENTO® Part-Skim Ricotta Cheese

2 eggs, beaten

2 cups chopped fresh spinach or 10 ounces frozen spinach, thawed and squeezed dry

½ teaspoon salt

¼ teaspoon black pepper

¼ teaspoon nutmeg

¼ teaspoon Italian seasoning or dried oregano

8 ounces portobello mushrooms, thinly sliced

4 cups (32 ounces) marinara pasta sauce, divided

8 ounces no cook lasagna noodles, divided

2 cups (8 ounces) SARGENTO® Shredded Mozzarella Cheese, divided

8 slices SARGENTO® Deli Style Sliced Provolone Cheese

1 cup (4 ounces) SARGENTO® ARTISAN BLENDS™ Shredded Parmesan Cheese

COMBINE Ricotta cheese, eggs, spinach, salt, pepper, nutmeg and Italian seasoning in small bowl; set aside.

COOK mushroom slices in nonstick pan coated with cooking spray over medium-low heat 5 minutes or until softened and lightly browned.

SPOON 1½ cups sauce into 13×9-inch baking dish; top with half of lasagna noodles and Ricotta mixture. Top with mushrooms and 1 cup Mozzarella cheese, then remaining noodles. Top with remaining sauce, remaining Mozzarella cheese, Provolone cheese and Parmesan cheese.

COVER with foil. Bake in preheated 350°F oven 45 minutes. Remove foil; bake 15 minutes more or until cheese is lightly browned. Let stand 15 minutes before serving. *Makes 8 servings*

Prep Time: 30 minutes
Cook Time: 60 minutes

Whole Wheat Spaghetti with Cauliflower & Feta

3 tablespoons olive oil
1 onion, chopped
4 cloves garlic, minced
1 head cauliflower, cut into bite-size florets
⅔ cup white wine or water
1 teaspoon salt
½ teaspoon black pepper
8 ounces uncooked whole wheat spaghetti
1 pint grape tomatoes, cut in half
½ cup coarsely chopped walnuts
¼ teaspoon red pepper flakes (optional)
½ cup crumbled feta cheese

1. Heat oil in large skillet over medium heat. Add onion; cook and stir 3 minutes or until soft. Add garlic; cook and stir 2 minutes. Add cauliflower; cook and stir 5 minutes. Add wine, salt and pepper. Cover and cook about 15 minutes or until cauliflower is crisp-tender.

2. Meanwhile, cook pasta according to package directions. Drain and keep warm; reserve ½ cup pasta cooking water.

3. Add tomatoes, walnuts and reserved pasta water to skillet; season with pepper flakes, if desired. Cook 2 to 3 minutes or until tomatoes begin to soften.

4. Toss spaghetti with vegetable sauce in skillet or serving bowl; top with feta.

Makes 4 servings

Vegan Variation: Omit feta cheese or substitute Dairy-Free Feta (page 202).

Ziti Ratatouille

1 large eggplant, peeled and cut into ½-inch cubes (about 1½ pounds)

2 medium zucchini, cut into ½-inch cubes

1 green or red bell pepper, cut into ½-inch pieces

1 large onion, chopped

4 cloves garlic, minced

1 jar (about 24 ounces) marinara sauce

2 cans (about 14 ounces each) diced tomatoes with garlic and onions

1 can (6 ounces) pitted black olives, drained

1 package (8 ounces) ziti pasta

Shredded Parmesan cheese (optional)

Slow Cooker Directions

1. Combine eggplant, zucchini, bell pepper, onion, garlic, marinara sauce and tomatoes in slow cooker. Cover and cook on LOW 4½ hours.

2. Stir in olives and pasta. Cover; cook 25 minutes or until pasta is tender. Sprinkle with Parmesan cheese, if desired. *Makes 6 to 8 servings*

Three Cheese Baked Ziti

1 container (15 ounces) part-skim ricotta cheese

2 eggs, beaten

¼ cup grated Parmesan cheese

1 box (16 ounces) ziti pasta, cooked and drained

1 jar (1 pound 10 ounces) RAGÚ® Chunky Pasta Sauce

1 cup shredded mozzarella cheese (about 4 ounces)

1. Preheat oven to 350°F. In large bowl, combine ricotta cheese, eggs and Parmesan cheese; set aside.

2. In another bowl, thoroughly combine pasta and Pasta Sauce.

3. In 13×9-inch baking dish, spoon ½ of the pasta mixture; evenly top with ricotta cheese mixture, then remaining pasta mixture. Sprinkle with mozzarella cheese. Bake 30 minutes or until heated through. Serve, if desired, with additional heated pasta sauce. *Makes 8 servings*

Vegetarian Rice Noodles

½ cup soy sauce

⅓ cup sugar

¼ cup lime juice

2 fresh red Thai chili peppers *or* 1 large jalapeño pepper, finely chopped

8 ounces thin rice noodles (rice vermicelli)

¼ cup vegetable oil

8 ounces firm tofu, drained and cut into triangles

1 jicama (8 ounces), peeled and chopped *or* 1 can (8 ounces) sliced water chestnuts, drained

2 medium sweet potatoes (1 pound), peeled and cut into ¼-inch-thick slices

2 large leeks, cut into ¼-inch-thick slices

¼ cup chopped unsalted dry-roasted peanuts

2 tablespoons chopped fresh mint

2 tablespoons chopped fresh cilantro

1. Combine soy sauce, sugar, lime juice and peppers in small bowl; set aside.

2. Place noodles in medium bowl. Cover with hot water; let stand 15 minutes or until soft. Drain well and cut into 3-inch lengths.

3. Meanwhile, heat oil in wok or large skillet over medium-high heat. Add tofu; cook 4 minutes or until both sides are golden. Remove with slotted spatula to baking sheet lined with paper towels.

4. Add jicama; stir-fry 5 minutes or until lightly browned; remove to baking sheet. Cook sweet potatoes in batches until tender and browned; remove to baking sheet. Add leeks. Stir-fry 1 minute.

5. Stir soy sauce mixture; add to wok. Heat until sugar dissolves. Add noodles; toss to coat. Gently stir in tofu, vegetables, peanuts, mint and cilantro.   *Makes 4 servings*

Cheese Ravioli with Wild Mushroom Sauce

2 tablespoons olive oil

1 medium onion, chopped

1 clove garlic, minced

8 ounces firm tofu, drained and crumbled

1½ cups ricotta cheese

1 cup grated Parmesan cheese, divided

½ teaspoon dried rosemary

¼ teaspoon salt

64 wonton wrappers (about 1⅓ packages)

Wild Mushroom Sauce (recipe follows)

1. Heat oil in small skillet over medium heat. Add onion and garlic; cook and stir 5 minutes or until tender. Place in medium bowl.

2. Process tofu, ricotta cheese, ⅓ cup Parmesan cheese, rosemary and salt in food processor until smooth. Stir into onion mixture.

3. Place 8 wonton wrappers on work surface; keep remaining wrappers covered with plastic wrap. Place about 1 tablespoon cheese mixture in center of each wrapper; brush edges with water. Place 8 wrappers over filling and press edges together to seal. Cover with plastic wrap and set aside. Repeat with remaining wrappers and filling. Prepare Wild Mushroom Sauce; keep warm.

4. Bring large saucepan of water to a simmer over medium-high heat. Cook ravioli in batches 3 to 4 minutes or until they float to surface. Remove with slotted spoon to warm platter. Serve with Wild Mushroom Sauce and sprinkle with remaining ⅔ cup Parmesan cheese. *Makes 6 to 8 servings*

Wild Mushroom Sauce

3 tablespoons olive oil

12 ounces shiitake or porcini mushrooms, sliced

6 ounces cremini or button mushrooms, sliced

1½ cups sliced green onions

1 tablespoon dried basil

½ to 1 teaspoon dried thyme

3 cups vegetable broth, divided
1 tablespoon cornstarch
2 tablespoons minced parsley
½ teaspoon salt
4 to 6 dashes hot pepper sauce

1. Heat oil in large skillet over medium heat. Add mushrooms, green onions, basil and thyme; cook and stir 10 to 15 minutes or until or until mushrooms brown and liquid evaporates. Add 2¾ cups broth; bring to a boil. Reduce heat to medium-low; simmer, 10 to 12 minutes or until broth is reduced by one third.

2. Stir cornstarch into remaining ¼ cup broth in small cup until smooth. Add to mushroom mixture. Bring to a boil, stirring constantly, 1 to 2 minutes or until thickened. Stir in parsley, salt and pepper sauce. *Makes about 3 cups*

Tofu Rigatoni Casserole

½ (16-ounce) package uncooked rigatoni pasta (3 cups)

4 cups loosely packed baby spinach

1 cup soft tofu

1 egg

¼ teaspoon salt

¼ teaspoon black pepper

¼ teaspoon ground nutmeg (optional)

1 can (about 14 ounces) diced tomatoes with basil, garlic and oregano

1 can (about 14 ounces) quartered artichokes, drained and chopped

2 cups (8 ounces) shredded Italian cheese blend, divided

1. Preheat oven to 350°F. Spray 11×7-inch baking dish with nonstick cooking spray.

2. Cook rigatoni in large saucepan according to package directions. Stir in spinach in bunches during last 2 minutes of cooking; cook until wilted. Drain; return to saucepan.

3. Meanwhile, combine tofu, egg, salt, pepper and nutmeg, if desired, in medium bowl; mix until blended. Fold tofu mixture into rigatoni. Add tomatoes, artichokes and 1½ cups cheese; mix well. Spoon into prepared baking dish.

4. Bake 20 minutes or until bubbly. Top with remaining ½ cup cheese. Bake 10 minutes or until cheese is browned.

Makes 6 servings

Three-Pepper Fettuccine

1 each red bell pepper, yellow bell pepper and jalapeño pepper

1 tablespoon olive oil

½ teaspoon chopped fresh thyme *or* ¼ teaspoon dried thyme

⅛ teaspoon salt, plus extra for cooking pasta

   Black pepper

1 package (9 ounces) refrigerated fresh fettuccine noodles

3 ounces mild goat cheese, crumbled

2 tablespoons minced chives or green onions

1. Preheat broiler. Broil peppers on foil-lined baking sheet or broiler pan, turning occasionally, until peppers are charred all over. Place peppers in a bowl. Cover with plastic wrap; let steam at least 10 minutes.

2. Remove charred skin; core and seed bell peppers. Cut into thin strips. Place in salad bowl. Core, seed and mince jalapeño. Add to peppers. Stir in olive oil, thyme, ⅛ teaspoon salt and black pepper. Set aside.

3. Meanwhile, cook fettuccine according to package directions. Drain well. Add fettuccine to peppers. Toss well. Add crumbled goat cheese. Toss again. Sprinkle with chives.   *Makes 4 servings*

Vegan Variation: Replace goat cheese with crumbled tofu.

Spinach Stuffed Manicotti

1 package (10 ounces) frozen spinach
8 uncooked manicotti shells
1½ teaspoons olive oil
1 teaspoon dried rosemary
1 teaspoon dried sage
1 teaspoon dried oregano
1 teaspoon dried thyme
1 teaspoon chopped garlic
1½ cups chopped fresh tomatoes
½ cup ricotta cheese
½ cup fresh whole wheat bread crumbs
2 egg whites, lightly beaten

1. Cook spinach according to package directions. Place in colander to drain. Let stand until cool enough to handle. Squeeze to remove excess moisture. Set aside.

2. Cook pasta according to package directions; drain. Rinse under cold running water until cool enough to handle; drain.

3. Preheat oven to 350°F.

4. Heat oil in medium saucepan over medium heat. Cook and stir rosemary, sage, oregano, thyme and garlic about 1 minute. Do not let herbs turn brown. Add tomatoes; reduce heat to low. Simmer, uncovered, 10 minutes, stirring occasionally.

5. Combine spinach, ricotta cheese and bread crumbs in bowl. Fold in egg whites. Spoon spinach mixture into shells.

6. Place one third of tomato mixture in 13×9-inch baking dish. Arrange manicotti in dish. Pour remaining tomato mixture over top. Cover with foil. Bake 30 minutes or until bubbly.

Makes 4 servings

Southwestern Corn & Pasta Casserole

2 tablespoons vegetable oil
1 red bell pepper, chopped
1 onion, chopped
1 jalapeño pepper,* minced
1 clove garlic, minced
1 cup sliced mushrooms
2 cups frozen corn
½ teaspoon salt
¼ teaspoon ground cumin
¼ teaspoon chili powder
4 ounces whole wheat elbow macaroni, cooked and drained
1½ cups milk
1 tablespoon unsalted butter
1 tablespoon all-purpose flour
1 cup (4 ounces) shredded pepper jack cheese
1 slice whole wheat bread, cut into ½-inch pieces

Jalapeño peppers can sting and irritate the skin, so wear rubber gloves when handling peppers and do not touch your eyes.

1. Preheat oven to 350°F. Grease 3-quart glass baking dish.

2. Heat oil in large skillet over medium-high heat. Add bell pepper, onion, jalapeño and garlic; cook and stir 5 minutes. Add mushrooms; cook and stir 5 minutes. Add corn, salt, cumin and chili powder. Reduce heat to low; simmer 5 minutes or until corn thaws. Stir in macaroni; set aside.

3. Bring milk to a simmer in small saucepan. Melt butter in large saucepan. Whisk in flour and cook 1 to 2 minutes. Gradually stir in milk. Cook and stir over medium-low heat until slightly thickened. Gradually stir in cheese. Cook and stir over low heat until cheese melts. Stir macaroni mixture into cheese sauce; mix well.

4. Spoon into prepared baking dish. Sprinkle bread pieces over casserole. Bake 20 to 25 minutes or until bubbly. Let stand 5 minutes before serving.   *Makes 4 servings*

Skillet Vegetable Lasagna

2¾ cups SWANSON® Vegetable Broth (Regular or Certified Organic)

15 uncooked oven-ready (no-boil) lasagna noodles

1 can (10¾ ounces) CAMPBELL'S® Condensed Cream of Mushroom Soup (Regular or 98% Fat Free)

1 can (about 14.5 ounces) diced tomatoes, undrained

1 package (10 ounces) frozen chopped spinach, thawed and well drained

1 cup ricotta cheese

1 cup shredded mozzarella cheese (about 4 ounces)

1. Heat the broth in a 12-inch skillet over medium-high heat to a boil. Break the noodles into pieces and add to the broth. Reduce the heat to low. Cook for 3 minutes or until the noodles are tender.

2. Stir the soup, tomatoes and spinach in the skillet. Cook for 5 minutes or until the mixture is hot and bubbling.

3. Remove the skillet from the heat. Spoon the ricotta cheese on top and sprinkle with the mozzarella cheese.   *Makes 4 servings*

Kitchen Tip: You can try using 4 ounces mozzarella cut into very thin slices instead of the shredded mozzarella.

Cook Time: 15 minutes
Prep Time: 10 minutes
Total Time: 25 minutes

Baked Ravioli with Pumpkin Sauce

1 package (9 ounces) refrigerated cheese ravioli
1 tablespoon butter
1 shallot, finely chopped
1 cup whipping cream
1 cup solid-pack pumpkin
½ cup shredded Asiago cheese, divided
½ teaspoon salt
¼ teaspoon ground nutmeg
⅛ teaspoon black pepper
½ cup coarse plain dry bread crumbs or small croutons

1. Preheat oven to 350°F. Grease 2-quart baking dish. Cook ravioli according to package directions. Drain well; cover and keep warm.

2. Meanwhile, melt butter in medium saucepan over medium heat. Add shallot; cook and stir 3 minutes or until tender. Reduce heat to low. Add cream, pumpkin, ¼ cup Asiago cheese, salt, nutmeg and pepper; cook and stir 2 minutes or until cheese melts. Gently stir in ravioli.

3. Transfer ravioli and sauce to prepared baking dish. Combine remaining ¼ cup Asiago cheese and bread crumbs in small bowl; sprinkle over ravioli.

4. Bake 15 minutes or until heated through and topping is lightly browned.

Makes 4 servings

Tip Refrigerated ravioli cooks in a matter of a few minutes, so keep a careful watch. It's better to undercook a little in this case since you will be baking the ravioli after the initial cooking.

Cauliflower Mac & Gouda

1 package (about 16 ounces) bowtie pasta

4 cups milk

2 cloves garlic, peeled and crushed

¼ cup (½ stick) plus 3 tablespoons butter, divided

5 tablespoons all-purpose flour

1 pound Gouda cheese, shredded

1 teaspoon ground mustard

⅛ teaspoon smoked paprika or regular paprika

    Salt and black pepper

1 head cauliflower, cored and cut into florets

1 cup panko bread crumbs

1. Cook pasta according to package directions until almost tender. Drain pasta, reserving water to cook cauliflower. Keep pasta warm.

2. Bring milk and garlic to a boil in small saucepan. Reduce heat; keep warm. Discard garlic.

3. Melt ¼ cup butter in large saucepan over medium heat; whisk in flour. Cook 1 minute, whisking constantly. Gradually add milk, whisking after each addition. Bring to a boil. Reduce heat; cook and stir 10 minutes or until thickened. Remove from heat.

4. Add cheese, mustard and paprika to sauce mixture; whisk until melted. Season with salt and pepper. Keep warm.

5. Preheat broiler. Bring pasta water to a boil; add cauliflower. Cook 3 to 5 minutes or just until tender; drain. Toss pasta and cauliflower with sauce mixture. Spoon pasta mixture into individual broilerproof dishes or 13×9-inch baking dish.

6. Melt remaining 3 tablespoons butter in small saucepan over medium heat. Add panko; stir just until moistened. Sprinkle over pasta. Broil 2 minutes or until golden brown.

Makes 6 to 8 servings

Baked Pasta with Ricotta

1 package (16 ounces) uncooked rigatoni or penne pasta

1 container (15 ounces) ricotta cheese

⅔ cup grated Parmesan cheese

2 eggs, lightly beaten

½ teaspoon salt

⅛ teaspoon black pepper

2 jars (26 ounces each) marinara sauce, divided

3 cups (12 ounces) shredded mozzarella cheese, divided

1. Preheat oven to 375°F. Spray 13×9-inch baking dish with nonstick cooking spray.

2. Cook rigatoni according to package directions; drain. Meanwhile, beat ricotta, Parmesan, eggs, salt and pepper in medium bowl until well blended.

3. Spread 2 cups marinara sauce over bottom of prepared dish; spoon half of cooked pasta over sauce. Top with half of ricotta mixture and 1 cup mozzarella. Repeat layers of marinara sauce, pasta, ricotta mixture and 1 cup mozzarella. Top with remaining marinara sauce and 1 cup mozzarella.

4. Cover with foil; bake about 1 hour or until bubbly. Uncover and bake about 5 minutes more or until cheese is completely melted. Let stand 15 minutes before serving.

Makes 8 servings

Tip Ricotta is a fresh cheese (not aged) so is quite perishable and should be used within a week after opening the container. In Italian the word ricotta means "recooked." Originally ricotta was made by recooking the whey left over from the production of sheep, cow or goat milk cheeses. American ricotta is made from whole or reduced-fat cow milk and is a bit moister and sweeter than the traditional version.

Grains & Legumes

Spicy Chickpeas & Couscous

1 can (about 14 ounces) vegetable broth
1 teaspoon ground coriander
½ teaspoon ground cardamom
½ teaspoon turmeric
½ teaspoon hot pepper sauce
¼ teaspoon salt
⅛ teaspoon ground cinnamon
1 cup julienned carrots
1 can (15 ounces) chickpeas, rinsed and drained
1 cup frozen green peas
1 cup uncooked couscous
2 tablespoons chopped fresh mint or parsley

1. Combine vegetable broth, coriander, cardamom, turmeric, pepper sauce, salt and cinnamon in large saucepan; bring to a boil over high heat. Add carrots; reduce heat and simmer 5 minutes.

2. Add chickpeas and green peas. Simmer, uncovered, 2 minutes.

3. Stir in couscous. Cover; remove from heat. Let stand 5 minutes or until liquid is absorbed. Sprinkle with mint.   *Makes 6 servings*

Polenta Lasagna

4¼ cups water, divided

1½ cups whole grain yellow cornmeal

  4 teaspoons finely chopped fresh marjoram

  1 tablespoon olive oil

  1 pound fresh mushrooms, sliced

  1 cup chopped leeks

  1 clove garlic, minced

½ cup (2 ounces) shredded mozzarella cheese

  2 tablespoons chopped fresh basil

  1 tablespoon chopped fresh oregano

⅛ teaspoon black pepper

  2 medium red bell peppers, chopped

¼ cup freshly grated Parmesan cheese, divided

1. Bring 4 cups of water to a boil in medium saucepan over high heat. Slowly add cornmeal to water, stirring constantly. Reduce heat to low; stir in marjoram. Simmer 15 to 20 minutes or until polenta thickens and pulls away from side of pan. Spread on 13×9-inch ungreased baking sheet. Cover and chill about 1 hour or until firm.

2. Heat oil in medium nonstick skillet over medium heat. Cook and stir mushrooms, leeks and garlic 5 minutes or until vegetables are crisp-tender. Stir in mozzarella, basil, oregano and black pepper.

3. Place bell peppers and remaining ¼ cup water in food processor or blender; cover and process until smooth. Preheat oven to 350°F. Spray 11×7-inch baking dish with nonstick cooking spray.

4. Cut cold polenta into twelve squares; arrange six squares in bottom of prepared dish. Spread with half of bell pepper mixture, half of vegetable mixture and 2 tablespoons Parmesan. Repeat layers. Bake 20 minutes or until cheese is melted and polenta is golden brown. *Makes 6 servings*

Winter Squash Risotto

2 tablespoons olive oil

1 small butternut squash or medium delicata squash, peeled and cut into
    1-inch pieces (about 2 cups)

1 large shallot or small onion, finely chopped

½ teaspoon paprika

½ teaspoon salt

¼ teaspoon dried thyme

¼ teaspoon black pepper

1 cup uncooked arborio rice

¼ cup dry white wine (optional)

4 to 5 cups hot vegetable broth

½ cup grated Parmesan or Romano cheese

1. Heat oil in large skillet over medium heat. Add squash; cook and stir 3 minutes. Add shallot; cook and stir 3 to 4 minutes or until squash is almost tender. Stir in paprika, salt, thyme and pepper. Add rice; stir to coat with oil.

2. Add wine, if desired; cook and stir until wine evaporates. Add ½ cup broth; cook, stirring occasionally. When rice is almost dry, stir in another ½ cup broth. Continue to stir rice occasionally, adding ½ cup broth each time previous addition is absorbed. Rice is done when consistency is creamy and grains are tender with slight resistance. (Total cooking time will be 20 to 30 minutes.)

3. Sprinkle with Parmesan cheese. Serve immediately.   *Makes 4 to 6 servings*

Vegan Variation: Omit Parmesan cheese, or replace it with a dairy-free alternative.

Southwestern Corn & Beans

1 tablespoon olive oil

1 large onion, diced

1 or 2 jalapeño peppers,* chopped

1 clove garlic, minced

2 cans (about 15 ounces each) red kidney beans, rinsed and drained

1 bag (16 ounces) frozen corn, thawed

1 can (about 14 ounces) diced tomatoes

1 green bell pepper, cut into 1-inch pieces

2 teaspoons chili powder

¾ teaspoon salt

½ teaspoon ground cumin

½ teaspoon black pepper

Jalapeño peppers can sting and irritate the skin, so wear rubber gloves when handling peppers and do not touch your eyes.

Slow Cooker Directions

1. Heat oil in medium skillet over medium heat. Add onion, jalapeño pepper and garlic; cook and stir 5 minutes. Transfer to slow cooker.

2. Add beans, corn, tomatoes, bell pepper, chili powder, salt, cumin and black pepper to slow cooker; mix well. Cover; cook on LOW 7 to 8 hours or on HIGH 2 to 3 hours.

Makes 6 servings

Serving Suggestion: For a party, spoon this colorful vegetarian dish into hollowed-out bell peppers or bread bowls.

Lentil Patties with Coconut-Mango Relish

1¼ cups dried lentils, sorted and rinsed
   Coconut-Mango Relish (page 147)
 1 small onion, chopped
 2 cloves garlic, minced
 ½ teaspoon cumin
 ¼ teaspoon salt
 ¼ teaspoon black pepper
 ⅛ teaspoon hot pepper sauce
 1 small carrot, shredded
 ¼ cup all-purpose flour
 1 egg
 2 tablespoons chopped pitted black olives
   Vegetable oil

1. Place lentils in 2-quart saucepan; cover with 2 inches of water. Bring to a boil; reduce heat to low. Cover and simmer 30 to 40 minutes or until tender; drain. Spread lentils on baking sheet lined with paper towels. Let stand about 20 minutes or until lentils are cool and most of moisture has been absorbed. Meanwhile, prepare Coconut-Mango Relish; set aside.

2. Combine half of lentils, onion, garlic, cumin, salt, pepper and hot pepper sauce in food processor; process until just combined.

3. Add carrot, flour, egg and olives. Process until well blended; transfer to large bowl. Stir in remaining half of lentils with spoon.

4. Coat bottom of large skillet with oil. Heat over medium-high heat. Shape 2 rounded tablespoonfuls of lentil mixture into patty. Repeat with remaining lentil mixture. Cook patties over medium heat 6 to 7 minutes on each side until browned on both sides, adding additional oil if needed. Serve with Coconut-Mango Relish.

Makes 4 to 6 servings

Coconut-Mango Relish

½ cup shredded coconut
½ cup fresh cilantro
2 tablespoons fresh ginger
2 tablespoons fresh lemon juice
1 tablespoon water
½ cup chopped mango

Place all ingredients except mango in food processor; process until finely chopped. Stir in mango. Cover; refrigerate up to 4 hours before serving.   *Makes 1½ cups*

Barley & Swiss Chard Skillet Casserole

1 cup water
1 cup chopped red bell pepper
1 cup chopped green bell pepper
¾ cup quick-cooking barley
⅛ teaspoon garlic powder
⅛ teaspoon red pepper flakes
2 cups packed coarsely chopped Swiss chard*
1 cup canned navy beans, rinsed and drained
1 cup quartered cherry tomatoes
¼ cup chopped fresh basil leaves
1 tablespoon olive oil
2 tablespoons Italian-seasoned dry bread crumbs

Fresh spinach or beet greens can be substituted for Swiss chard.

1. Preheat broiler.

2. Bring water to a boil in large ovenproof skillet; add bell peppers, barley, garlic powder and red pepper flakes. Reduce heat; cover and simmer 10 minutes or until liquid is absorbed and barley is tender. Remove from heat.

3. Stir in chard, beans, tomatoes, basil and olive oil. Sprinkle with bread crumbs. Broil 2 minutes or until golden.   *Makes 4 servings*

Black Bean & Rice Stuffed Poblano Peppers

2 large or 4 small poblano peppers
½ (15½-ounce) can black beans, rinsed and drained
½ cup cooked brown rice
⅓ cup chunky salsa
⅓ cup shredded Cheddar cheese or pepper jack cheese, divided

1. Preheat oven to 375°F. Spray shallow baking pan with olive oil cooking spray.

2. Cut thin slice from one side of each pepper. Chop pepper slices; set aside. In medium saucepan, cook whole peppers in boiling water 6 minutes. Drain and rinse with cold water. Remove and discard seeds and membranes.

3. Stir together beans, rice, salsa, chopped pepper and ¼ cup cheese. Spoon into peppers; place peppers in prepared pan. Cover with foil. Bake 12 to 15 minutes or until heated through.

4. Sprinkle with remaining cheese. Bake 2 minutes more or until cheese melts.

Makes 2 servings

Tabbouleh

½ cup fine-grain bulgur wheat
½ cup hot water
¼ cup extra virgin olive oil
1 tablespoon lemon juice
1½ cups peeled, seeded and diced cucumbers
1½ cups diced tomatoes (3 medium tomatoes)
1 cup chopped Italian parsley
¼ cup chopped green onions
¼ cup chopped fresh mint leaves
1 teaspoon chopped garlic
Salt to taste

Place bulgur in medium bowl; cover with hot water. Let stand 20 to 30 minutes or until liquid is absorbed. Stir in olive oil and lemon juice. Add remaining ingredients. Chill at least 2 hours, stirring occasionally.

Makes 6 servings

Lentil Stew over Couscous

3 cups dried lentils (1 pound), sorted and rinsed

3 cups water

1 can (about 14 ounces) vegetable broth

1 can (about 14 ounces) diced tomatoes

1 large onion, chopped

1 green bell pepper, chopped

4 stalks celery, chopped

1 medium carrot, sliced

2 cloves garlic, chopped

1 teaspoon dried marjoram

¼ teaspoon black pepper

1 tablespoon olive oil

1 tablespoon cider vinegar

4½ to 5 cups hot cooked couscous

Slow Cooker Directions

1. Combine lentils, water, broth, tomatoes, onion, bell pepper, celery, carrot, garlic, marjoram and black pepper in slow cooker; stir. Cover and cook on LOW 8 to 9 hours or until vegetables are tender.

2. Stir in oil and vinegar. Serve over couscous. *Makes 12 servings*

 *Tip* Brown lentils are the most common variety, but a trip to an Indian market will introduce you to dozens of kinds of "dal", the Indian word for lentils. Red lentils, which are sold split to reveal their gaudy orange insides, are one of the most popular, since they cook very quickly to become soft and creamy. There are also yellow lentils, black lentils, split mung beans and more! Most lentils can be used interchangeably although cooking times will vary, as will the texture of the finished dish.

Vegetarian Paella

2 teaspoons vegetable oil
1 cup chopped onion
2 cloves garlic, minced
1 cup uncooked brown rice
2¼ cups vegetable broth
1 teaspoon salt
1 teaspoon Italian seasoning
½ teaspoon ground turmeric
⅛ teaspoon ground red pepper
1 can (14½ ounces) stewed tomatoes
1 cup chopped red bell pepper
1 cup coarsely chopped carrots
1 can (14 ounces) quartered artichoke hearts, drained
1 zucchini, halved lengthwise and sliced
½ cup frozen baby peas

1. Heat oil in 10-inch nonstick skillet over medium-high heat. Add onion and garlic; cook and stir 6 to 7 minutes or until tender. Reduce heat to low and stir in rice. Cook over medium heat 1 minute, stirring constantly.

2. Add broth, salt, Italian seasoning, turmeric and ground red pepper. Bring to a boil. Reduce heat to medium-low. Simmer, covered, 30 minutes. Stir in tomatoes, bell pepper and carrots. Simmer, covered, 10 minutes more. Reduce heat to low and stir in artichoke hearts, zucchini and peas. Cook, covered, about 10 minutes or until vegetables are crisp-tender.   *Makes 6 servings*

Barley, Bean & Corn Frittata

2 cups water
½ cup uncooked pearl barley
¾ teaspoon salt, divided
2 teaspoons olive oil
1 can (about 15 ounces) black beans, rinsed and drained
2 cups (8 ounces) shredded Cheddar cheese, divided
¾ cup corn
½ cup chopped green bell pepper
¼ cup chopped fresh cilantro
7 eggs
1 cup cottage cheese
½ teaspoon ground red pepper
1 cup medium salsa

1. Bring water to a boil in medium saucepan over high heat. Add barley and ¼ teaspoon salt. Reduce heat to low. Cover and simmer 40 to 45 minutes or until tender. Remove from heat. Let stand, covered, 5 minutes. Drain.

2. Preheat oven to 400°F. Brush 10-inch cast iron or other ovenproof skillet with olive oil. Layer barley, beans, 1 cup Cheddar cheese, corn, bell pepper and cilantro in skillet. Blend eggs, cottage cheese, remaining ½ teaspoon salt and ground red pepper in blender or food processor just until smooth. Pour egg mixture over layers.

3. Bake 30 minutes or until egg mixture is set. Sprinkle with remaining 1 cup Cheddar cheese. Bake 5 minutes or until cheese is melted. Spoon salsa evenly over top. Let stand 5 minutes before cutting into wedges. *Makes 6 to 8 servings*

Taco Rice and Beans

2 tablespoons olive oil
1 medium onion, diced
1 cup water
1 packet (1.25 ounces) ORTEGA® Taco Seasoning Mix
1 can (15 ounces) ORTEGA® Black Beans, drained
2 cups cooked rice
¼ cup ORTEGA® Thick & Chunky Salsa

Heat oil in skillet over medium heat until hot. Add onion. Cook and stir 3 minutes. Add water and seasoning mix. Cook and stir until combined and slightly thickened. Stir in beans, rice and salsa. Cook 5 minutes longer or until heated through.

Makes 4 servings

Tip: For a great meal, fold Taco Rice and Beans into an Ortega soft flour tortilla.

Prep Time: 5 minutes
Start to Finish: 15 minutes

Minted Multigrain Salad

1½ cups peeled, quartered and sliced cucumbers
1 cup cooked quinoa (½ cup dry)
1 cup cooked medium bulgur wheat
1 cup California Ripe Olives, cut into wedges
½ cup cooked wheat berries (¼ cup dry)
½ cup (2 ounces) crumbled feta cheese (omit for vegan)
2 tablespoons lemon juice
¼ cup chopped mint
½ teaspoon ground cumin
Salt to taste (optional)

In a large mixing bowl, combine cucumbers, quinoa, bulgur, California Ripe Olives and wheat berries. Gently toss in feta cheese, lemon juice, mint, cumin and salt, if desired. Cover and chill for 15 minutes before serving.

Makes 4 servings

Favorite recipe from *California Olive Industry*

Quinoa & Roasted Corn

1 cup uncooked quinoa

2 cups water

½ teaspoon salt

4 ears corn *or* 2 cups frozen corn

¼ cup plus 1 tablespoon vegetable oil, divided

1 cup chopped green onions, divided

1 teaspoon coarse salt

1 cup quartered grape tomatoes or chopped plum tomatoes, drained*

1 cup black beans, rinsed and drained

¼ teaspoon grated lime peel

Juice of 1 lime (about 2 tablespoons)

¼ teaspoon sugar

¼ teaspoon cumin

¼ teaspoon black pepper

Place tomatoes in strainer and place over bowl 10 to 15 minutes.

1. Place quinoa in fine-mesh strainer; rinse well under cold running water. Transfer to medium saucepan; add water and ½ teaspoon salt. Bring to a boil over high heat. Reduce heat; cover and simmer 15 to 18 minutes or until water is absorbed and quinoa is tender. Transfer quinoa to large bowl.

2. Meanwhile, remove husks and silk from corn; cut kernels off cobs. Heat ¼ cup oil in large skillet over medium-high heat. Add corn; cook 10 to 12 minutes or until tender and light brown, stirring occasionally. Stir in ⅔ cup green onions and coarse salt; cook and stir 2 minutes. Add corn to quinoa. Gently stir in tomatoes and black beans.

3. Combine lime peel, lime juice, sugar, cumin and black pepper in small bowl. Whisk in remaining 1 tablespoon oil until blended. Pour over quinoa mixture; toss lightly to coat. Sprinkle with remaining ⅓ cup green onions. Serve warm or chilled.

Makes 6 to 8 servings

Barley & Pear-Stuffed Acorn Squash

    3 small acorn or carnival squash
    2 cups vegetable broth
    ¾ teaspoon salt, divided
    1 cup quick-cooking barley
    2 tablespoons butter
    1 small onion, chopped
    1 stalk celery, chopped
    ¼ teaspoon black pepper
    1 large unpeeled ripe pear, diced
    ½ cup chopped hazelnuts, toasted*
    ¼ cup maple syrup
    ½ teaspoon ground cinnamon

To toast hazelnuts, spread in single layer on a baking sheet. Bake in a preheated 350°F oven 7 to 10 minutes or until golden, stirring occasionally.

1. Pierce each squash with knife in several places. Microwave on HIGH 12 to 14 minutes or until tender, turning once. Let stand 5 minutes. Cut squash in half lengthwise; scoop out seeds. Arrange halves, cut side up, in large baking dish.

2. Meanwhile, bring broth and ½ teaspoon salt to a boil in large saucepan over high heat. Stir in barley; reduce heat to low. Cover; simmer 12 minutes or until tender. (Do not drain.)

3. Preheat oven to 350°F.

4. Melt butter in large skillet over medium heat. Add onion, celery, remaining ¼ teaspoon salt and pepper; cook and stir 5 minutes. Add pear; cook 5 minutes. Stir in barley, hazelnuts, maple syrup and cinnamon. Spoon barley mixture into squash.

5. Cover with foil. Bake 15 to 20 minutes or until heated through.

Makes 6 servings

Barley & Apple-Stuffed Acorn Squash: Substitute one apple for the pear and walnuts for the hazelnuts.

Note: Squash can be stuffed ahead of time. Prepare as directed in steps 1 through 4. Cool; tightly cover and refrigerate. To serve, bake at 350°F 25 to 30 minutes or until heated through.

Wheat Berry Apple Salad

1 cup uncooked wheat berries (whole wheat kernels)
½ teaspoon salt
2 unpeeled apples (1 red and 1 green)
½ cup dried cranberries
⅓ cup chopped walnuts
1 stalk celery, chopped
Grated peel and juice of 1 medium orange
2 tablespoons rice wine vinegar
1½ tablespoons chopped fresh mint
Lettuce leaves (optional)

1. Place wheat berries and salt in large saucepan; cover with 1 inch of water.* Bring to a boil. Stir and reduce heat to low. Cover and cook, stirring occasionally, 45 minutes to 1 hour or until wheat berries are tender but chewy. (Add additional water if wheat berries become dry during cooking.) Drain and let cool. (Refrigerate for up to 4 days if not using immediately.)

2. Cut apples into bite-size pieces. Combine wheat berries, apples, cranberries, walnuts, celery, orange peel, orange juice, vinegar and mint in large bowl. Cover; refrigerate at least 1 hour to allow flavors to blend. Serve on lettuce leaves.

Makes about 6 cups

To cut cooking time by 20 to 30 minutes, soak wheat berries in water overnight. Drain and cover with 1 inch of fresh water before cooking.

Tip Wheat berries are whole wheat kernels with the bran and germ still intact. They take a while to cook but are easy to love. The flavor is mild, earthy and nutty and the texture is chewy and satisfying. Wheat berries are nutritional champions, too, and are packed with fiber, protein and iron.

Hot & Hearty

Black Bean & Mushroom Chilaquiles

2 tablespoons olive oil

1 medium onion, chopped

1 medium green bell pepper, chopped

1 jalapeño or serrano pepper,* seeded and minced

2 cans (about 15 ounces each) black beans, rinsed and drained

1 can (about 14 ounces) diced tomatoes

10 ounces white mushrooms, cut into quarters

1½ teaspoons ground cumin

1½ teaspoons dried oregano

1 cup (4 ounces) shredded sharp Cheddar cheese, plus additional for garnish

6 cups tortilla chips

Jalapeño and serrano peppers can sting and irritate the skin, so wear rubber gloves when handling peppers and do not touch your eyes.

Slow Cooker Directions

1. Heat oil in medium skillet over medium heat. Add onion, bell pepper and jalapeño. Cook, stirring occasionally, until onion softens. Transfer to slow cooker. Add beans, tomatoes, mushrooms, cumin and oregano. Cover; cook on LOW 6 hours or on HIGH 3 hours.

2. Sprinkle Cheddar cheese over bean mixture. Cover; cook until cheese melts. Stir to combine.

3. Coarsely crush tortilla chips. Top with black bean mixture and sprinkle with additional cheese.

Makes 6 servings

Eggplant Parmigiana

     2 eggs, beaten
   ¼ cup milk
       Dash garlic powder
       Dash onion powder
       Dash salt
       Dash black pepper
   ½ cup seasoned dry bread crumbs
     1 large eggplant (about 1½ pounds), cut into ½-inch-thick slices
       Vegetable oil
     1 jar (about 26 ounces) pasta sauce
     4 cups (16 ounces) shredded mozzarella cheese
  2½ cups (10 ounces) shredded Swiss cheese
   ¼ cup grated Parmesan cheese
   ¼ cup grated Romano cheese

1. Preheat oven to 350°F. Combine eggs, milk, garlic powder, onion powder, salt and pepper in shallow dish. Place bread crumbs in another shallow dish. Dip eggplant into egg mixture; coat with bread crumbs.

2. Heat ¼ inch oil in large skillet over medium-high heat. Brown eggplant on both sides in batches; drain on paper towels.

3. Spread ¼ cup pasta sauce in bottom of 13×9-inch baking dish. Layer half of eggplant, half of mozzarella cheese, half of Swiss cheese and half of remaining sauce in dish. Repeat layers. Sprinkle with Parmesan and Romano cheeses.

4. Bake 30 minutes or until heated through and cheeses are melted.

Makes 4 servings

Nut Roast

1½ cups unsalted walnuts, pecans, almonds or cashews
2 tablespoons olive oil
1 onion, finely chopped
4 ounces cremini mushrooms (about 6 large), sliced
2 cloves garlic, minced
1 can (about 14 ounces) diced tomatoes
1 cup old-fashioned oats
2 eggs, lightly beaten
2 tablespoons all-purpose flour
1 tablespoon chopped fresh sage
1 tablespoon chopped fresh parsley
1 teaspoon chopped fresh thyme
Salt and pepper

1. Spray 8-inch loaf pan with nonstick cooking spray. Preheat oven to 350°F. Place nuts in food processor. Pulse until finely chopped, allowing some larger pieces to remain. Transfer to large bowl.

2. Heat oil in medium skillet over medium heat. Add onion, mushrooms and garlic; cook and stir 3 minutes or until softened. Transfer mixture to bowl with nuts.

3. Stir in tomatoes, oats, eggs, flour, sage, parsley, thyme, salt and pepper until combined. Spoon mixture into prepared pan. Bake 45 to 50 minutes or until firm and browned. Cool slightly before slicing. *Makes 6 to 8 servings*

Vegan Variation: Replace eggs with a vegan egg substitute.

Tip Nut roasts are classic vegetarian dishes that are often served as an alternative to meat entrées for Thanksgiving or other festive occasions. This rich and satisfying main course can be accompanied by tomato or cranberry sauce if you like. You can also customize the ingredients to suit your taste by substituting your favorite nuts, herbs and spices.

Vegetable Risotto

2 tablespoons olive oil, divided
1 medium zucchini, cubed
1 medium yellow squash, cubed
1 cup sliced stemmed shiitake mushrooms
1 cup chopped onion
1 clove garlic, minced
3 plum tomatoes, seeded and chopped
1 teaspoon dried oregano
3 cups vegetable broth
1 cup arborio rice
¼ cup grated Parmesan cheese
   Salt and black pepper (optional)
½ cup frozen peas, thawed

1. Heat 1 tablespoon oil in large saucepan over medium heat. Add zucchini and yellow squash; cook and stir 5 minutes or until crisp-tender. Transfer to medium bowl; set aside.

2. Add mushrooms, onion and garlic to saucepan; cook and stir 5 minutes or until tender. Add tomatoes and oregano; cook and stir 2 to 3 minutes or until tomatoes are soft. Transfer to bowl with zucchini mixture.

3. Heat broth in small saucepan over medium-low heat; keep hot.

4. Meanwhile, heat remaining 1 tablespoon oil in large saucepan over medium heat. Add rice; cook and stir 2 minutes.

5. Using ladle or measuring cup, add about ¾ cup broth to rice. Cook and stir until broth is absorbed. Repeat with remaining broth. Cook until rice is tender but not mushy. Total cooking time will be 20 to 25 minutes.

6. Stir cheese into rice mixture. Season to taste with salt and pepper, if desired. Stir in reserved vegetables and peas; cook until heated through. Serve immediately.

Makes 4 to 6 servings

Vegan Variation: Omit Parmesan cheese or replace with a dairy-free alternative.

Seitan Fajitas

2 packages (8 ounces each) seitan,* sliced
1 packet (1 ounce) fajita seasoning, dissolved according to package directions
1 tablespoon vegetable oil
1 red bell pepper, sliced
½ medium onion, sliced
1 package (8 ounces) sliced mushrooms
6 (6- to 7-inch) tortillas, warmed
  Salsa and guacamole (optional)

Seitan is a meat substitute made from wheat gluten. See page 27 of the introduction for more information.

1. Place seitan in large resealable food storage bag. Pour seasoning mixture over seitan. Seal bag; shake to coat.

2. Heat oil in large skillet. Add pepper and onion; cook and stir 4 to 5 minutes or until crisp-tender. Add mushrooms; cook and stir 1 to 2 minutes or until mushrooms are softened. Add seitan and seasoning mixture; cook and stir 1 to 2 minutes or until seitan is heated through and vegetables are coated with seasoning. Divide vegetable mixture evenly among tortillas. Serve with salsa and guacamole.   *Makes 6 fajitas*

Creamy Artichoke & Spinach Casserole

½ cup finely chopped onion
½ cup (1 stick) butter
2 packages (10 ounces each) frozen chopped spinach, thawed and squeezed dry
1 can (14 ounces) artichoke hearts, drained and quartered
1½ cups plain yogurt
½ cup (2 ounces) grated Wisconsin Parmesan cheese
½ teaspoon salt
¼ teaspoon black pepper

In medium skillet, sauté onion in butter until tender; add remaining ingredients. Mix together; spread in 1½-quart casserole. Bake at 350°F 25 minutes.

Makes 8 servings

Favorite recipe from *Wisconsin Milk Marketing Board*

Hot Three-Bean Casserole

2 tablespoons olive oil

1 cup coarsely chopped onion

1 cup chopped celery

2 cloves garlic, minced

1 can (about 15 ounces) chickpeas, rinsed and drained

1 can (about 15 ounces) kidney beans, rinsed and drained

1 cup coarsely chopped tomato

1 can (about 8 ounces) tomato sauce

1 cup water

1 to 2 jalapeño peppers,* minced

1 tablespoon chili powder

2 teaspoons sugar

1½ teaspoons ground cumin

1 teaspoon salt

1 teaspoon dried oregano

¼ teaspoon black pepper

2½ cups (10 ounces) frozen cut green beans

Jalapeño peppers can sting and irritate the skin, so wear rubber gloves when handling peppers and do not touch your eyes.

1. Heat oil in large skillet over medium heat. Add onion, celery and garlic; cook and stir 5 minutes or until tender.

2. Add chickpeas, kidney beans, tomato, tomato sauce, water, jalapeño pepper, chili powder, sugar, cumin, salt, oregano and black pepper. Bring to a boil. Reduce heat to low; simmer, uncovered, 20 minutes. Add green beans; simmer 10 minutes or until tender.

Makes 12 servings

Vegetable Pizza Primavera

½ recipe New York-Style Pizza Crust (recipe follows)
1½ cups broccoli florets
1 carrot, shredded
1 small yellow squash or zucchini, cut into ¼-inch-thick slices
6 thin asparagus spears, cut into 1½-inch pieces
10 fresh pea pods
1 green onion, thinly sliced
¾ cup (3 ounces) shredded Swiss cheese or provolone cheese
⅓ cup slivered fresh basil leaves
¼ cup grated Romano cheese
Black pepper
½ teaspoon olive oil

1. Prepare New York-Style Pizza Crust dough. Move oven rack to lowest position and preheat oven to 500°F.

2. Place steamer rack in large saucepan. Add water to about ¼ inch below rack. Bring water to a boil over high heat. Add broccoli; cover and steam 6 to 8 minutes or until crisp-tender. Lift broccoli from pan and plunge into large bowl of ice water until chilled. Repeat with remaining vegetables except green onion, adding water to saucepan as needed. Steam carrots 3 to 4 minutes, squash 2 minutes, asparagus 3 to 4 minutes, pea pods 1 minute. Drain vegetables and pat dry with paper towels.

3. Sprinkle Swiss cheese over dough, leaving 1-inch border. Bake 3 to 4 minutes or until cheese melts and crust is light golden. Place all vegetables on pizza. Top with basil, Romano cheese and pepper. Bake 4 to 6 minutes or until crust is deep golden and cheese is melted. Brush edge of crust with olive oil. *Makes 2 to 4 servings*

New York-Style Pizza Crust

⅔ cup warm water (110° to 115°F)
1 teaspoon sugar
1 teaspoon active dry yeast
1¾ cups all-purpose or bread flour
½ teaspoon salt

1. Combine water and sugar in small bowl; stir to dissolve sugar. Sprinkle yeast over water; stir. Let stand 5 to 10 minutes or until foamy.

2. Combine flour and salt in medium bowl. Stir in yeast mixture until soft dough forms. Place dough on lightly floured surface. Knead 5 minutes or until dough is smooth and elastic, adding additional flour, 1 tablespoon at a time, as needed. Place dough in oiled medium bowl. Turn dough to coat top. Cover; let rise in warm place 30 minutes or until doubled.

3. Punch dough down; place on lightly floured surface and knead 2 minutes or until smooth. Divide dough in half. Pat each half into flat disc. Let rest 2 to 3 minutes. (Wrap well and refrigerate or freeze half of dough for later use if making only one pizza.)

4. Pat and gently stretch dough into 10- to 11-inch circle allowing it to rest for a few minutes if it becomes hard to stretch. Transfer to baking sheet sprayed with nonstick cooking spray or to pizza peel. Proceed as recipe directs.

Makes 2 thin 10- to 11-inch crusts

Italian Eggplant with Millet & Pepper Stuffing

¼ cup uncooked millet

2 small eggplants (about ¾ pound total)

¼ cup chopped red bell pepper, divided

¼ cup chopped green bell pepper, divided

1 teaspoon olive oil

1 clove garlic, minced

1½ cups vegetable broth

½ teaspoon ground cumin

½ teaspoon dried oregano

⅛ teaspoon red pepper flakes

1. Cook and stir millet in large heavy skillet over medium heat 5 minutes or until golden. Transfer to small bowl; set aside.

2. Cut eggplants lengthwise into halves. Scoop out flesh, leaving about ¼-inch-thick shell. Reserve shells; chop eggplant flesh. Combine 1 teaspoon red bell pepper and 1 teaspoon green bell pepper in small bowl; set aside.

3. Heat oil in same skillet over medium heat. Add chopped eggplant, remaining red and green bell pepper and garlic; cook and stir about 8 minutes or until eggplant is tender.

4. Stir in toasted millet, broth, cumin, oregano and red pepper flakes. Bring to a boil over high heat. Reduce heat to medium-low. Cook, covered, 35 minutes or until all liquid has been absorbed and millet is tender. Remove from heat; let stand, covered, 10 minutes.

5. Preheat oven to 350°F. Pour 1 cup water into 8-inch square baking pan. Fill eggplant shells with millet mixture. Sprinkle with reserved chopped bell peppers, pressing in lightly. Carefully place filled shells in prepared pan. Bake 15 minutes or until heated through. *Makes 4 servings*

Roasted Vegetable Tacos

    Olive oil nonstick cooking spray
 1 cup sliced fresh mushrooms (3 ounces)
 1 medium onion, cut into wedges
 1 medium red bell pepper, cut lengthwise into eighths
 1 medium zucchini, cut into ¼-inch slices
 1 packet (1.25 ounces) ORTEGA® Taco Seasoning Mix
 ½ teaspoon salt
 ¼ teaspoon crushed red pepper
 1 cup (4 ounces) shredded Cheddar or Monterey Jack cheese
12 ORTEGA® Yellow Corn Taco Shells
 ¾ cup ORTEGA® Salsa, any variety
    Chopped fresh cilantro (optional)

Preheat oven to 425°F. Coat jelly-roll pan (15½×10½×1-inch) with nonstick cooking spray.

Place mushrooms, onion, bell pepper and zucchini in single layer in pan. Coat with nonstick cooking spray. Sprinkle with seasoning mix, salt and red pepper. Bake, uncovered, 20 to 25 minutes or until tender, turning vegetables once.

Sprinkle cheese into taco shells. Top with vegetable mixture and salsa. Sprinkle with cilantro, if desired.

Makes 6 servings

Note: Try roasting different vegetables, such as eggplant, potatoes or yellow summer squash.

Prep Time: 15 minutes
Start to Finish: 40 minutes

Barley & Vegetable Risotto

4½ cups vegetable broth
2 teaspoons olive oil
1 small onion, diced
8 ounces sliced mushrooms
¾ cup uncooked pearl barley
1 large red bell pepper, diced
2 cups packed baby spinach
¼ cup grated Parmesan cheese
¼ teaspoon black pepper

1. Bring broth to a boil in medium saucepan. Reduce heat to low to keep broth hot.

2. Meanwhile, heat oil in large saucepan over medium heat. Add onion; cook and stir 4 minutes. *Increase heat to medium-high.* Add mushrooms; cook and stir 5 minutes or until mushrooms begin to brown and liquid evaporates.

3. Add barley; cook 1 minute. Add ¼ cup broth; cook and stir about 2 minutes or until broth is almost all absorbed. Continue adding broth, ¼ cup at a time, stirring constantly. After 20 minutes, stir in bell pepper. When barley is almost tender (about 30 minutes total), stir in spinach. Cook and stir 1 minute or until spinach wilts. Stir in cheese and black pepper.

Makes 4 servings

Vegan Variation: Omit Parmesan cheese or replace with a dairy-free alternative.

Tip Choose your favorite kind of mushrooms for this recipe or use a mixture of button, cremini, shiitake and oyster. Cremini mushrooms, which are also called Italian brown or baby bellas, are closely related to the common white button mushroom. They have a richer, slightly earthier flavor. Fresh mushrooms should be used as soon as possible and refrigerated in a paper bag, never in plastic.

Chiles Rellenos Casserole

 3 eggs, separated
¾ cup all-purpose flour
¾ cup milk
½ teaspoon salt
 1 tablespoon butter
½ cup chopped onion
 2 cans (7 ounces each) whole green chiles, drained
 8 slices (1 ounce each) Monterey Jack cheese, cut into halves
    Toppings: sour cream, sliced green onions, sliced olives, guacamole and salsa

1. Preheat oven to 350°F. Grease 13×9-inch baking dish.

2. Combine egg yolks, flour, milk and salt in food processor or blender; process until smooth. Place in large bowl; set aside.

3. Melt butter in small skillet over medium heat. Add onion; cook and stir until tender.

4. Pat chiles dry with paper towels. Slit each chile lengthwise and carefully remove seeds. Place 2 halves of cheese and 1 tablespoon onion in each chile; reshape chiles to cover cheese. Place in single layer in prepared baking dish.

5. Beat egg whites in medium bowl until soft peaks form; fold into yolk mixture. Pour over chiles in baking dish.

6. Bake 20 to 25 minutes or until casserole is puffed and knife inserted into center comes out clean. Broil 4 inches from heat 30 seconds or until top is golden brown. Serve with desired toppings.

Makes 4 servings

Vegetarian Orzo & Feta Bake

1 package (16 ounces) orzo pasta

1 can (4¼ ounces) chopped black olives, drained

2 cloves garlic, minced

1 can (about 14 ounces) diced Italian-style tomatoes

1 can (about 14 ounces) vegetable broth

2 tablespoons olive oil

6 to 8 ounces feta cheese, cut into ½-inch cubes

1. Preheat oven to 450°F.

2. Combine orzo, olives and garlic in large baking dish. Stir in tomatoes, broth and oil. Top with cheese.

3. Cover with foil. Bake 22 to 24 minutes or until pasta is tender. Remove from oven; let stand 5 minutes.

Makes 6 servings

Italian Vegetarian Grill

1 large bell pepper, cut into strips
1 medium zucchini, cut into ½-inch thick pieces
½ pound asparagus (about 10 spears)
1 red onion, cut into ½-inch-thick rounds
¼ cup olive oil
1 teaspoon salt, divided
½ teaspoon Italian seasoning
½ teaspoon black pepper, divided
4 cups water
1 cup uncooked polenta or cornmeal
4 ounces goat cheese

1. Arrange bell peppers, zucchini and asparagus in single layer on baking sheet. To hold onion together securely, pierce slices horizontally with metal skewers. Add to baking sheet. Combine oil, ½ teaspoon salt, Italian seasoning and ¼ teaspoon black pepper in small bowl. Brush mixture generously over vegetables, turning to coat all sides.

2. Prepare grill for direct cooking. Meanwhile, bring water to a boil with remaining ½ teaspoon salt in large saucepan. Whisk in polenta gradually. Reduce heat to medium. Cook, stirring constantly, until polenta thickens and begins to pull away from side of pan. Stir in polenta and remaining ¼ teaspoon black pepper. Keep warm.

3. Grill vegetables over medium-high heat, covered, 10 to 15 minutes or until tender, turning once. Place bell peppers in large bowl. Cover; let stand 5 minutes to loosen skin. When cool enough to handle, peel off charred skin. Cut all vegetables into bite-size pieces.

4. Serve polenta topped with vegetables and sprinkled with goat cheese.

Makes 4 servings

Vegan Variation: Omit the goat cheese or replace it with crumbled tofu or toasted bread crumbs.

7-Layer Meatless Tortilla Pie

2 cans (about 15 ounces each) pinto beans, rinsed and drained
1 cup PACE® Picante Sauce
¼ teaspoon garlic powder or 1 clove garlic, minced
2 tablespoons chopped fresh cilantro leaves
1 can (about 15 ounces) black beans, rinsed and drained
1 small tomato, chopped (about ½ cup)
7 flour tortillas (8-inch)
8 ounces shredded Cheddar cheese (about 2 cups)

1. Mash the pinto beans in a medium bowl with a fork. Stir in **¾ cup** picante sauce and the garlic powder.

2. Stir the remaining picante sauce, cilantro, black beans and tomato in a medium bowl.

3. Place **1** tortilla onto a baking sheet. Spread **¾ cup** pinto bean mixture over the tortilla to within ½ inch of the edge. Top with **¼ cup** cheese. Top with **1** tortilla and **⅔ cup** black bean mixture. Top with **¼ cup** cheese. Repeat the layers twice more. Top with the remaining tortilla and spread with the remaining pinto bean mixture. Cover with aluminum foil.

4. Bake at 400°F. for 40 minutes or until the filling is hot. Uncover the pie. Top with the remaining cheese. Cut the pie into 6 wedges. Serve with additional picante sauce and sprinkle with additional cilantro, if desired. *Makes 6 servings*

Prep Time: 20 minutes
Cook Time: 40 minutes
Total Time: 1 hour

Salads & Sandwiches

Veggie Salad with White Beans & Feta Cheese

1 can (about 15 ounces) navy beans, rinsed and drained

1 can (14 ounces) quartered artichoke hearts, drained

1 medium green bell pepper, chopped

1 yellow bell pepper, chopped

1 cup grape tomatoes, halved

¼ cup chopped fresh basil *or* 1½ tablespoons dried basil plus ¼ cup chopped fresh parsley

¼ cup extra virgin olive oil

3 to 4 tablespoons red wine vinegar

1 clove garlic, minced

1 teaspoon Dijon mustard

½ teaspoon black pepper

¼ teaspoon salt

4 ounces crumbled feta cheese with sun-dried tomatoes and basil

1 package (about 5 ounces) spring greens mix (optional)

Combine beans, artichokes, bell peppers, tomatoes, basil, oil, vinegar, garlic, mustard, pepper and salt in large bowl; toss gently. Fold in cheese. Let stand 10 minutes. Serve over greens, if desired.

Makes 4 servings

Vegan Variation: Omit the feta cheese or replace it with Dairy-Free "Feta" (recipe on page 202.)

Portobello Provolone Panini

6 to 8 ounces sliced portobello mushrooms

⅓ cup plus 1 tablespoon olive oil, divided

3 tablespoons balsamic vinegar

1 clove garlic, minced

½ teaspoon salt

¼ teaspoon black pepper

1 loaf (16 ounces) ciabatta or Italian bread *or* 4 ciabatta rolls

8 ounces sliced provolone cheese

¼ cup chopped fresh basil

8 ounces plum tomatoes, thinly sliced

3 tablespoons whole grain Dijon mustard

1. Place mushrooms, ⅓ cup oil, vinegar, garlic, salt and pepper in large resealable food storage bag. Seal tightly; shake to coat mushrooms evenly. Let stand 15 minutes, turning frequently. (Mushrooms may be prepared up to 24 hours in advance; refrigerate and turn occasionally.)

2. Preheat indoor grill. Brush both sides of bread with remaining 1 tablespoon oil; slice bread in half lengthwise.

3. Arrange mushrooms evenly over bottom half of cut bread; drizzle with marinade. Top with cheese, basil and tomatoes. Spread mustard evenly over cut side of remaining half of bread; place over tomatoes. Cut sandwich into four equal pieces. Grill each sandwich 8 minutes or until bread is golden and cheese is melted. Wrap each sandwich tightly in foil to keep warm or serve at room temperature.

Makes 4 servings

Quinoa & Mango Salad

1 cup uncooked quinoa*

2 cups water

2 cups cubed peeled mango (about 2 large mangoes)

½ cup sliced green onions

½ cup dried cranberries

2 tablespoons chopped fresh parsley

¼ cup olive oil

1 tablespoon plus 1½ teaspoons white wine vinegar

1 teaspoon Dijon mustard

½ teaspoon salt

⅛ teaspoon black pepper

*Pronounced keen-wah. For more information see page 21 of the introduction.

1. Place quinoa in fine mesh strainer; rinse well. Transfer to medium saucepan and add water. Bring to a boil. Reduce heat; simmer, covered, 10 to 12 minutes until all water is absorbed. Stir; let stand, covered, 15 minutes. Transfer to large bowl; cover and refrigerate at least 1 hour.

2. Add mango, green onions, cranberries and parsley to quinoa; mix well.

3. Combine oil, vinegar, mustard, salt and pepper in small bowl; whisk until blended. Pour over quinoa mixture; mix until well blended. *Makes 8 servings*

Tip: This salad can be made several hours ahead and refrigerated. Allow it to stand at room temperature for at least 30 minutes before serving.

Tip Quinoa is usually rinsed before using. The seeds are naturally coated with a substance called saponin, which protects quinoa from insects while it's growing. The grain is rinsed once before packaging to remove the bitter saponin, but it doesn't hurt to rinse it again. Place quinoa in a fine-mesh strainer and swish the grains around under cold running water. If the water looks cloudy or soapy, that's the saponin.

Tempeh Melt

3 teaspoons hamburger seasoning

1 teaspoon paprika

1 package (8 ounces) unseasoned soy tempeh*

4 slices Swiss cheese

4 to 8 slices pumpernickel or marble rye bread

   Thousand Island Sauce (recipe follows)

   Dill pickle slices or sauerkraut

   Onion slices or caramelized red onion

*For more information see page 26 of the introduction.

1. Combine 1 cup water, hamburger seasoning and paprika in large deep skillet over high heat. Cut tempeh in half crosswise; add to skillet and bring to a boil. Reduce heat; simmer 20 minutes, turning tempeh occasionally. Remove tempeh from skillet; cut each piece in half.

2. Preheat grill to medium-high. Grill tempeh, covered, 4 minutes per side. Top with cheese; cook 30 seconds or until cheese melts. Spread 1 tablespoon sauce over one piece of bread; top with tempeh, pickles, onion and another piece of bread.

Makes 4 servings

Thousand Island Sauce: Combine ½ cup mayonnaise, ½ cup chili sauce, 1 tablespoon sweet pickle relish, 2 teaspoons Dijon mustard and dash ground red pepper in food processor. Process until almost smooth.

Tip

Tempeh is a fermented soy food that originated in Indonesia hundreds of years ago. It's best to cook tempeh before eating it, although this is for taste reasons rather than food safety ones. Cooking improves both flavor and texture. Like tofu, tempeh has an ability to readily absorb flavors and cooking enhances this. Its firm texture makes it a great choice to cook on the grill or use in a sandwich.

Greek Salad with Dairy-Free "Feta"

Dairy-Free "Feta"

    1 package (about 14 ounces) firm or extra firm tofu
    ½ cup extra virgin olive oil
    ¼ cup lemon juice
    2 teaspoons salt
    ½ teaspoon black pepper
    2 teaspoons Greek or Italian seasoning
    1 teaspoon onion powder
    ½ teaspoon garlic powder

Salad

    1 small red onion, cut into thin slices
    1 pint grape tomatoes, halved
    1 yellow bell pepper, cut into slivers
    2 seedless cucumbers, sliced

1. Cut tofu crosswise into two pieces, each about 1 inch thick. Place on cutting board lined with paper towels; top with layer of paper towels. Place weighted baking dish on top of tofu. Press for 30 minutes. Pat tofu dry and crumble into large bowl.

2. Combine oil, lemon juice, salt, pepper and Greek seasoning in small jar with lid; shake to combine well. Reserve ¼ cup of mixture for salad dressing. Add onion powder and garlic powder to remaining mixture. Pour over tofu and toss gently. Refrigerate overnight or for at least 2 hours.

3. Combine tomatoes, cucumbers, bell pepper, and onion in serving bowl. Add tofu "feta" and reserved dressing. Toss gently.   *Makes 4 to 6 servings*

Mediterranean Pita Sandwiches

1 cup plain yogurt

1 tablespoon chopped fresh cilantro

2 cloves garlic, minced

1 teaspoon lemon juice

1 can (about 15 ounces) chickpeas, rinsed and drained

1 can (14 ounces) artichoke hearts, rinsed, drained and coarsely chopped

1½ cups thinly sliced cucumbers

½ cup shredded carrots

½ cup chopped green onions

4 rounds whole wheat pita bread, cut in half

1. Combine yogurt, cilantro, garlic and lemon juice in small bowl.

2. Combine chickpeas, artichoke hearts, cucumbers, carrots and green onions in medium bowl. Stir in yogurt mixture until well blended.

3. Divide salad among pita halves.

Makes 4 servings

Barbecue Tofu

1 package (14 ounces) extra firm tofu

1 bottle (18 ounces) barbecue sauce

4 to 6 pieces frozen Texas toast, prepared according to package directions
   Coleslaw

1. Place tofu on paper-towel lined plate; cover with another paper towel. Place weighted saucepan or baking dish on top of tofu. Press 15 minutes. Cut tofu into 8 equal slices.

2. Spread half of barbecue sauce in large saucepan; arrange tofu slices over sauce in single layer. Cover with remaining sauce. Cover; cook over medium heat about 10 minutes or until tofu is hot, carefully flipping tofu after 5 minutes.

3. Serve tofu on top of Texas toast. Drizzle with sauce; serve with coleslaw.

Makes 4 to 6 servings

Chickpea Burgers

  1 can (15 ounces) chickpeas, rinsed and drained
  ⅓ cup chopped carrots
  ⅓ cup herbed croutons
  ¼ cup chopped fresh parsley
  ¼ cup chopped onion
  1 egg white
  1 teaspoon minced garlic
  1 teaspoon grated lemon peel
  ½ teaspoon black pepper
  ¼ teaspoon salt
    Nonstick cooking spray
  4 whole grain hamburger buns
    Tomato slices, lettuce leaves and salsa

1. Place chickpeas, carrots, croutons, parsley, onion, egg white, garlic, lemon peel, pepper and salt in food processor; process until blended. Shape mixture into four patties.

2. Spray large nonstick skillet with cooking spray; heat over medium heat. Cook patties 4 to 5 minutes or until bottoms are browned. Spray tops of patties with cooking spray; turn and cook 4 to 5 minutes or until browned.

3. Serve burgers on buns with tomato, lettuce and salsa.   *Makes 4 servings*

Vegan Variation: Replace egg white with a dairy-free egg substitute.

Brown Rice, Asparagus & Tomato Salad

  1 cup instant brown rice
 12 spears fresh asparagus, cooked and cut into pieces
  2 medium tomatoes
2½ teaspoons lemon juice
  2 teaspoons olive oil
 ⅛ teaspoon salt
 ⅛ teaspoon black pepper
 ¼ cup minced chives or green onions
  2 teaspoons minced fresh dill

1. Bring 1 cup water to a boil in medium saucepan. Stir in rice; bring to a boil. Cover; reduce heat to low. Simmer 5 minutes. Remove from heat. Stir rice; cover and set aside 5 minutes or until water is absorbed and rice is tender. Fluff with fork.

2. Meanwhile, place asparagus in large salad bowl. Core tomatoes over a separate bowl to catch juice. Dice tomatoes, reserving juice. Add tomatoes to asparagus. Stir together 1½ tablespoons reserved tomato juice, lemon juice, oil, salt and pepper in small bowl. Stir in chives and dill.

3. Add rice to salad bowl. Pour in dressing; toss gently.   *Makes 4 servings*

Instant brown rice has an almost identical nutritional profile to longer cooking regular brown rice, so feel free to substitute. Both instant and regular brown rice are much better for you than any kind of white rice. If you prefer the chewier, firmer texture of regular long grain brown rice, next time cook an extra large batch and freeze a cup or two for later use. It can easily be thawed in the microwave.

Meatless Sloppy Joes

2 cups thinly sliced onions

2 cups chopped green bell peppers

1 can (about 15 ounces) kidney beans, drained and mashed

1 can (8 ounces) tomato sauce

2 tablespoons ketchup

1 tablespoon yellow mustard

2 cloves garlic, finely chopped

1 teaspoon chili powder

Cider vinegar (optional)

2 sandwich rolls, halved

Slow Cooker Directions

Combine all ingredients except vinegar and rolls in slow cooker. Cover; cook on LOW 5 to 5½ hours or until vegetables are tender. Season to taste with cider vinegar, if desired. Serve on rolls.   *Makes 4 servings*

South Asian Curried Potato Salad

2 pounds unpeeled new potatoes

1½ teaspoons salt, divided

¾ cup plain yogurt (regular or dairy-free)

½ cup diced onion

½ cup diced celery

⅓ cup diced green bell pepper

¼ cup mayonnaise (regular or vegan)

2 teaspoons curry powder

2 teaspoons lemon juice

1. Place potatoes and 1 teaspoon salt in large saucepan; add cold water to cover. Bring to a boil; boil 20 minutes or just until potatoes are tender. Drain and cool.

2. Combine yogurt, onion, celery, bell pepper, mayonnaise, curry powder, lemon juice and remaining ½ teaspoon salt in large bowl; mix well.

3. Cut potatoes into 1-inch pieces. Add potatoes to yogurt mixture; stir gently to coat.

Makes 10 servings

Grilled Ratatouille Sandwich

⅓ cup olive oil

⅓ cup *French's*® Spicy Brown Mustard

1 tablespoon chopped fresh rosemary *or* 1 teaspoon dried rosemary

3 cloves garlic, minced

½ cup kalamata olives, pitted and chopped

½ small eggplant (about ¾ pound)

1 medium zucchini

1 large red onion

2 large ripe plum tomatoes

1 large red bell pepper

1 (12-inch) sourdough baguette, cut lengthwise in half (about 12 ounces)

1. Combine oil, mustard, rosemary and garlic in small bowl. Place olives in food processor; add 2 tablespoons mustard mixture. Cover and process until smooth; set aside. Reserve remaining mustard mixture.

2. Cut eggplant and zucchini lengthwise into ¼-inch-thick slices. Cut onion and tomatoes crosswise into ½-inch-thick slices. Cut red bell pepper lengthwise into 2-inch-wide pieces; discard seeds. Place vegetables on platter. Baste with reserved mustard mixture.

3. Place vegetables on oiled grid or vegetable basket. Grill over medium-high heat 3 to 5 minutes or until vegetables are tender, basting and turning once.

4. To serve, remove and discard excess bread from bread halves. Spread olive mixture on cut surfaces of bread. Layer vegetables on bottom half of bread; cover with top half. Cut crosswise into portions.   *Makes 4 servings*

Olive Tapenade Dip: Combine 1½ cups (10 ounces) kalamata olives, pitted; 3 tablespoons each olive oil and *French's*® Spicy Brown Mustard; 1 teaspoon minced dried rosemary and 1 clove garlic in food processor. Process until puréed. Serve with vegetable crudites. Makes about 1 cup dip.

Prep Time: 25 minutes
Cook Time: 5 minutes

French Lentil Salad

1½ cups dried brown or green lentils, rinsed and sorted
¼ cup chopped walnuts
4 green onions, finely chopped
3 tablespoons balsamic vinegar
2 tablespoons chopped fresh parsley
1 tablespoon olive oil
¾ teaspoon salt
½ teaspoon dried thyme
¼ teaspoon black pepper

1. Combine 2 quarts water and lentils in large saucepan; bring to a boil over high heat. Cover; reduce heat and simmer 30 minutes or until lentils are tender, stirring occasionally. Drain lentils.

2. Meanwhile, preheat oven to 375°F. Spread walnuts in even layer on baking sheet. Bake 5 minutes or until lightly browned. Cool completely on baking sheet.

3. Combine lentils, onions, vinegar, parsley, oil, salt, thyme and pepper in large bowl. Cover; refrigerate 1 hour or until cool.

4. Serve on lettuce leaves, if desired. Top with toasted walnuts before serving.

Makes 4 servings

 Rinsing and sorting lentils is necessary since they can contain bits of dirt and even small stones, which can look a lot like lentils. Chances are you won't find any foreign objects in the most lentils, since they are cleaned after harvesting. Still, it's worth a quick check for that one time in a dozen that there is something that needs to be removed.

Portobello & Fontina Sandwiches

2 teaspoons olive oil

2 large portobello mushrooms, stemmed

   Salt and black pepper

2 to 3 tablespoons sun-dried tomato pesto

4 slices crusty Italian bread

4 ounces fontina cheese, sliced

½ cup fresh basil leaves

   Additional olive oil

1. Preheat broiler. Line baking sheet with foil.

2. Drizzle 2 teaspoons oil over both sides of mushrooms; season with salt and pepper. Place mushrooms, gill sides up, on prepared baking sheet. Broil mushrooms 4 minutes per side or until tender. Cut into ¼-inch-thick slices.

3. Spread pesto evenly on two bread slices; layer with mushrooms, cheese and basil. Top with remaining bread slices. Brush outsides of sandwiches lightly with additional olive oil.

4. Heat large grill pan or skillet over medium heat. Add sandwiches; press down lightly with spatula or weigh down with small plate. Cook sandwiches 4 to 5 minutes per side or until cheese melts and sandwiches are golden brown. *Makes 2 sandwiches*

Tip Portobello mushrooms are the mature versions of cremini mushrooms. The open, flat cap of a portobello exposes the gills underneath. Some cooks scrape off the gills before preparing portobellos. This is not necessary, but the dark brown gills will color any liquid an unappetizing brownish-grey, so for a cream sauce or a soup, it's better to remove them. Portobello stems are edible, but are usually removed since they can be quite tough. Save them to flavor a stock or stew if you like.

Kohlrabi & Carrot Slaw

2 pounds kohlrabi bulbs, peeled and shredded
2 medium carrots, shredded
1 small red bell pepper, chopped
8 cherry tomatoes, cut into halves
2 green onions, thinly sliced
¼ cup mayonnaise
¼ cup plain yogurt
2 tablespoons cider vinegar
2 tablespoons finely chopped fresh parsley
1 teaspoon dried dill weed
¼ teaspoon salt
¼ teaspoon ground cumin
⅛ teaspoon black pepper

1. Combine kohlrabi, carrots, bell pepper, tomatoes and green onions in medium bowl.

2. Combine mayonnaise, yogurt, vinegar, parsley, dill, salt, cumin and black pepper in small bowl until smooth. Add to vegetables; toss to coat. Cover; refrigerate until ready to serve.

Makes 8 servings

Vegan Variation: Replace the mayonnaise with a vegan substitute and use a dairy-free yogurt.

Tip Kohlrabi is a milder, sweeter relative of the turnip. Choose a bulb that is heavy for its size without soft spots. In reality, the kohlrabi bulb is actually part of the plant's stem and grows above ground so it is sometimes called stem turnip. The color of kohlrabi may be white, green, purple or a combination. If the greens are still attached they may be cooked like turnip greens.

Grilled Vegetable & Hummus Muffaletta

1 small eggplant, cut lengthwise into ⅛-inch slices

1 yellow squash, cut lengthwise into ⅛-inch slices

1 small zucchini, cut on the diagonal into ⅛-inch slices

¼ cup extra virgin olive oil

½ teaspoon salt

¼ teaspoon black pepper

1 boule (8 inches), or round bread, cut in half horizontally

1 container (8 ounces) hummus, any flavor

1 jar (12 ounces) roasted red bell peppers, drained

1 jar (6 ounces) marinated artichoke hearts, drained and chopped

1 small tomato, thinly sliced

1. Preheat grill or grill pan. In large bowl, toss eggplant, squash and zucchini with oil, salt and pepper. Grill vegetables 2 to 3 minutes per side or until tender. Cool to room temperature.

2. Gently pull out some of the boule's interior, leaving about a 1½-inch shell. (Use leftover bread for bread crumbs.) Spread hummus evenly on inside bottom of bread. Layer grilled vegetables, peppers, artichokes and tomatoes inside bread. Place top back on bread. Wrap stuffed loaf tightly in plastic wrap. Chill well before slicing into wedges. *Makes 6 servings*

Party Perfect

Artichoke, Olive & Goat Cheese Pizza

½ recipe New York-Style Pizza Crust (recipe page 178)

2 teaspoons olive oil

2 teaspoons minced fresh rosemary leaves *or* 1 teaspoon dried rosemary

3 cloves garlic, minced

½ cup (2 ounces) shredded Monterey Jack cheese

½ cup water-packed artichoke hearts, sliced

4 sun-dried tomatoes, packed in oil, drained and sliced (about ½ cup)

2½ ounces soft goat cheese, sliced or crumbled

10 kalamata olives, pitted and halved (about ¼ cup)

1. Prepare New York-Style Pizza Crust dough. Preheat oven to 500°F.

2. Brush olive oil over prepared crust. Sprinkle with rosemary and garlic; brush again to coat with oil. Bake 3 to 4 minutes or until crust is light golden. Sprinkle with half of Monterey Jack cheese, leaving 1-inch border. Top with artichokes, tomatoes, goat cheese and olives. Sprinkle with remaining Monterey Jack cheese.

3. Bake 3 to 4 minutes or until crust is deep golden and cheese is melted.

Makes 2 to 4 servings

Cheese Soufflé

¼ cup (½ stick) butter
¼ cup all-purpose flour
¼ teaspoon salt
¼ teaspoon ground red pepper
⅛ teaspoon black pepper
1½ cups milk, warmed to room temperature
6 eggs, separated
1 cup (4 ounces) shredded Cheddar cheese
Pinch cream of tartar (optional)

1. Preheat oven to 375°F. Grease four individual 2-cup soufflé dishes or one 2-quart soufflé dish.

2. Melt butter in large saucepan over medium-low heat. Add flour; whisk 2 minutes or until mixture just begins to color. Whisk in milk gradually. Add salt, red pepper and black pepper. Whisk until mixture comes to a boil and thickens. Remove from heat.

3. Stir in egg yolks, one at a time, and cheese.

4. Meanwhile, place egg whites in clean large bowl with cream of tartar, if desired. Beat with electric mixer on high speed until egg whites form stiff peaks.

5. Fold egg whites into cheese mixture gently until almost combined. (Some streaks of white should remain.) Transfer mixture to prepared dish.

6. Bake about 20 minutes for small soufflés (30 to 40 minutes for larger soufflé) or until puffed and browned and wooden skewer inserted into center comes out moist but clean. Serve immediately. *Makes 4 servings*

Tip Soufflés have a reputation for being difficult to make, but don't let that put you off. The most common mistake is to deflate the egg whites by folding them in too completely. Any soufflé deflates within minutes after removing it from the oven so for maximum "wow" have your guests assembled and ready to eat.

Eggplant Crêpes with Roasted Tomato Sauce

    Roasted Tomato Sauce (recipe follows)
  2 eggplants (8 to 9 inches long), cut into 18 (¼-inch-thick) slices
    Olive oil cooking spray
  1 package (10 ounces) frozen chopped spinach, thawed and squeezed dry
  1 cup ricotta cheese
  ½ cup grated Parmesan cheese
 1¼ cups (5 ounces) shredded Gruyère* cheese
    Fresh oregano leaves (optional)

*Gruyère cheese is a Swiss cheese that has been aged for 10 to 12 months. Any Swiss cheese can be substituted.

1. Prepare Roasted Tomato Sauce. *Reduce oven temperature to 425°F.*

2. Arrange eggplant on nonstick baking sheets in single layer. Spray both sides of eggplant slices with cooking spray. Bake eggplant 10 minutes; turn and bake 5 to 10 minutes or until tender. Cool. *Reduce oven temperature to 350°F.*

3. Combine spinach, ricotta and Parmesan cheese; mix well. Spray 12×8-inch baking pan with cooking spray. Spread spinach mixture evenly on eggplant slices; roll up slices, beginning at short ends. Place rolls, seam side down, in baking dish.

4. Cover dish with foil. Bake 25 minutes. Uncover; sprinkle rolls with Gruyère cheese. Bake, uncovered, 5 minutes or until cheese is melted. Serve with Roasted Tomato Sauce. *Makes 4 to 6 servings*

Roasted Tomato Sauce

 20 ripe plum tomatoes (about 2⅔ pounds), cut in half and seeded
  3 tablespoons olive oil, divided
  ½ teaspoon salt
  ⅓ cup minced fresh basil
  ½ teaspoon black pepper

Preheat oven to 450°F. Toss tomatoes with 1 tablespoon oil and salt. Place, cut sides down, on nonstick baking sheet. Bake 20 to 25 minutes or until skins are blistered. Cool. Process tomatoes, remaining 2 tablespoons oil, basil and pepper in food processor until smooth. *Makes about 1 cup*

Guacamole Cones

    6 (6-inch) flour tortillas
    1 tablespoon vegetable oil
    1 teaspoon chili powder
    2 ripe avocados
  1½ tablespoons fresh lime juice
    1 tablespoon finely chopped green onion
    ¼ teaspoon salt
    ¼ teaspoon black pepper
      Dash hot pepper sauce (optional)
    2 to 3 plum tomatoes, chopped

1. Preheat oven to 350°F. Line baking sheet with parchment paper.

2. Cut tortillas in half. Roll each tortilla half into cone shape; secure with toothpick. Brush outside of each cone with oil; sprinkle lightly with chili powder. Place on prepared baking sheet.

3. Bake 9 minutes or until cones are lightly browned. Turn cones upside down; bake about 5 minutes or until golden brown on all sides. Cool cones 1 minute; remove toothpicks and cool completely.

4. Cut avocados in half; remove and discard pits. Scoop avocado pulp from skins and place in medium bowl; mash with fork. Stir in lime juice, green onion, salt, pepper and hot pepper sauce, if desired, until blended.

5. Fill bottom of each tortilla cone with about 1 tablespoon chopped tomato; top with small scoop of guacamole and additional chopped tomatoes. Serve immediately.

Makes 12 cones

Barbecue Seitan Skewers

1 package (8 ounces) cubed seitan*
½ cup barbecue sauce
1 red bell pepper, cut into 12 pieces
1 green bell pepper, cut into 12 pieces
12 mushrooms
1 zucchini, cut into 12 pieces

For more information see page 27 of the introduction.

1. Separate seitan into cubes; place in medium bowl. Add ¼ cup barbecue sauce; stir to coat. Marinate in refrigerator 30 minutes. Soak four bamboo skewers 20 minutes.

2. Oil grid; preheat grill to medium-high. Thread seitan, bell peppers, mushrooms and zucchini onto skewers. Grill, covered, 4 minutes per side or until seitan is hot and glazed with sauce, brushing with some of remaining sauce occasionally.

Makes 4 servings

Edamame Hummus

1 package (16 ounces) frozen shelled edamame, thawed
2 green onions, coarsely chopped (about ½ cup)
½ cup loosely packed fresh cilantro
3 to 4 tablespoons water
2 tablespoons canola oil
1½ tablespoons fresh lime juice
1 tablespoon honey (use sugar or agave nectar for vegan)
2 cloves garlic
1 teaspoon salt
¼ teaspoon black pepper
Rice crackers, baby carrots, cucumber slices and sugar snap peas

1. Combine edamame, green onions, cilantro, 3 tablespoons water, oil, lime juice, honey, garlic, salt and pepper in food processor; process until smooth. Add additional water to thin dip, if necessary.

2. Serve with crackers and vegetables for dipping.

Makes about 2 cups

Cheddar & Leek Strata

8 eggs, lightly beaten
2 cups milk
½ cup beer
2 cloves garlic, minced
¼ teaspoon salt
¼ teaspoon black pepper
1 loaf (16 ounces) sourdough bread, cut into ½-inch cubes
2 small leeks, coarsely chopped
1 red bell pepper, chopped
1½ cups (6 ounces) shredded Swiss cheese
1½ cups (6 ounces) shredded sharp Cheddar cheese

1. Combine eggs, milk, ale, garlic, salt and black pepper in large bowl. Beat until well blended.

2. Place half of bread cubes in greased 13×9-inch baking dish. Sprinkle half of leeks and half of bell pepper over bread cubes. Top with ¾ cup Swiss cheese and ¾ cup Cheddar cheese. Repeat layers. Pour egg mixture evenly over top.

3. Cover tightly with plastic wrap or foil. Weigh top of strata down with slightly smaller baking dish. Refrigerate strata at least 2 hours or overnight.

4. Preheat oven to 350°F. Bake, uncovered, 40 to 45 minutes or until center is set. Serve immediately.

Makes 12 servings

Tip Leeks look like giant green onions. Although related to both onions and garlic, leeks have a milder flavor. It's important to clean leeks thoroughly since dirt can hide inside the many tightly packed layers. Trim the top and bottom and slit the leek in half vertically. Wash the leek thoroughly, separating the layers under water to rinse away all the dirt and grit.

Spinach Gnocchi

2 packages (10 ounces) frozen chopped spinach

1 cup ricotta cheese

2 eggs

⅓ cup freshly grated Parmesan cheese

3 tablespoons all-purpose flour

½ teaspoon salt

⅛ teaspoon black pepper

⅛ teaspoon ground nutmeg

Marinara sauce

Shaved Parmesan cheese

1. Cook spinach according to package directions. Drain well; let cool. Squeeze spinach dry; place in medium bowl. Stir in ricotta cheese. Add eggs; mix well. Add ⅓ cup Parmesan cheese, 3 tablespoons flour, salt, pepper and nutmeg; mix. Cover; refrigerate 1 hour.

2. Press a heaping tablespoonful of spinach mixture between a spoon and your hand to form oval gnocchi; place on baking pan lined with parchment paper. Repeat with remaining spinach mixture. Freeze gnocchi 30 minutes.

3. Drop 8 to 12 gnocchi into large pot of boiling salted water; reduce heat to medium. Cook, uncovered, about 2½ minutes or until they float. Remove gnocchi with slotted spoon; drain on paper towels.

4. Serve gnocchi with marinara sauce. Top with shaved Parmesan cheese.

Makes 4 to 6 servings (about 32 gnocchi)

Vegetable Empanadas

  2 tablespoons olive oil
  1 cup frozen diced hash brown potatoes
  1 red bell pepper, chopped
  1 green bell pepper, chopped
  1 onion, chopped
  1 package (8 ounces) sliced mushrooms
  2 teaspoons minced garlic
1½ teaspoons ground cumin
  ½ teaspoon salt
  ½ teaspoon ground nutmeg
  ½ teaspoon black pepper
  ¼ teaspoon ground red pepper
  1 package (17 ounces) frozen puff pastry sheets, thawed
  ½ cup (2 ounces) shredded Monterey Jack cheese
  3 tablespoons milk
    Salsa

1. Heat oil in large nonstick skillet over medium heat. Add potatoes, bell peppers, onion, mushrooms, garlic and spices; cook and stir 5 minutes. Let cool to room temperature.

2. Preheat oven to 400°F. Unfold pastry sheets on floured surface. Roll each sheet into 12-inch square with lightly floured rolling pin; cut each square into four squares with sharp knife. Place about ¼ cup filling in corner of each square; sprinkle with 1 tablespoon cheese.

3. Brush small amount of milk on edges of pastry squares. Fold opposite corners over filling to meet each other, forming triangles. Press edges with fork to seal. Cut small slit in top of each triangle with knife. (Empanadas may be covered and refrigerated up to 24 hours or frozen up to 1 month.)

4. Place triangles on *ungreased* baking sheets; brush tops with remaining milk. Bake 15 to 20 minutes or until puffed and golden. Serve with salsa.   *Makes 8 servings*

Five Mushroom Risotto

4 cups vegetable broth

4 tablespoons olive oil, divided

2 tablespoons butter

1 shallot, minced

¼ cup fresh Italian parsley, minced

¼ cup dry white wine

2½ cups shiitake, chanterelle, portobello, oyster and/or button mushrooms, chopped into ½-inch pieces

½ teaspoon coarse salt

1 cup arborio rice

½ cup whipping cream

¼ cup grated Parmesan cheese

   Salt and black pepper

   White truffle oil (optional)

1. Bring broth to a boil in medium saucepan. Reduce heat to low; keep warm.

2. Heat 2 tablespoons oil and butter in deep saucepan or skillet over medium-high heat. Add shallot; cook and stir 30 seconds or just until beginning to brown. Add parsley; cook and stir 30 seconds.

3. Add wine; cook and stir until wine evaporates. Add mushrooms and coarse salt; cook and stir until mushrooms have softened and reduced their volume by half. Transfer mushroom mixture to medium bowl; set aside.

4. Heat remaining 2 tablespoons oil in same saucepan. Add rice; cook and stir 1 to 2 minutes or until edges of rice become translucent.

5. Reduce heat to medium-low. Add ½ cup broth, stirring constantly until broth is absorbed. Repeat until only ½ cup broth remains. Stir mushroom mixture into rice. Add remaining broth; cook and stir until absorbed.

6. Remove from heat; add cream and Parmesan cheese, stirring until cheese is melted. Season with salt and pepper. Drizzle with truffle oil, if desired. *Makes 4 servings*

Mediterranean Vegetable Bake

2 tomatoes, sliced

1 small red onion, sliced

1 medium zucchini, sliced

1 small eggplant, sliced

1 small yellow squash, sliced

1 large portobello mushroom, sliced

2 cloves garlic, finely chopped

3 tablespoons olive oil

2 teaspoons chopped fresh rosemary leaves

⅔ cup dry white wine

   Salt and black pepper

1. Preheat oven to 350°F. Grease bottom of oval casserole or 13×9-inch baking dish.

2. Arrange slices of vegetables in rows, alternating different types and overlapping slices in pan to make attractive arrangement; sprinkle evenly with garlic. Combine olive oil and rosemary in small bowl; drizzle over vegetables.

3. Pour wine over vegetables; season with salt and pepper. Cover loosely with foil. Bake 20 minutes. Uncover; bake 10 to 15 minutes or until vegetables are tender.

Makes 4 to 6 servings

Tip Rosemary is an herb that is best used in its fresh form. When it is dried the needle-shaped leaves of rosemary can be tough and sharp unless thoroughly crushed. Rosemary is traditionally a symbol of remembrance and friendship.

French Carrot Quiche

1 pound carrots
1 tablespoon butter, plus additional for greasing
¼ **cup chopped green onions**
½ **teaspoon herbes de Provence**
1 cup milk
¼ **cup heavy cream**
½ **cup flour**
2 eggs, lightly beaten
½ **teaspoon minced fresh thyme**
¼ **teaspoon ground nutmeg**
½ **cup (2 ounces) shredded Gruyère or Swiss cheese**

1. Peel carrots and cut into rounds. Butter four shallow 1-cup baking dishes or one 9-inch quiche dish or shallow casserole. Preheat oven to 350°F.

2. Melt butter in large skillet over medium heat. Cook and stir carrots, green onions and herbes de Provence 3 to 4 minutes or until carrots are tender.

3. Meanwhile, combine milk and cream in medium bowl; whisk in flour gradually. Stir in eggs, thyme and nutmeg.

4. Spread carrot mixture in prepared dishes; add milk mixture. Sprinkle with cheese. Bake 20 to 25 minutes for individual quiches (30 to 40 minutes for 9-inch quiche) or until firm. Serve warm or at room temperature.   *Makes 4 servings.*

Tip Buy only crisp, hard carrots. They should not be floppy, cracked or growing new leaves. The carrots labeled "baby" are usually cut and peeled from larger regular carrots. They are convenient, but dry out quickly and become bitter. Check out the many colors of carrots available from farmers' markets. They come in purple, maroon, yellow and white. Always remove the tops before storing carrots since they continue to draw moisture and nutrients from the root.

Sun-Dried Tomato Appetizer Torte

3 cups chopped onion

3 jars (about 7 ounces each) oil-packed sun-dried tomatoes, drained and finely chopped

3 tablespoons sugar

1 tablespoon minced garlic

1 piece (2 inches) fresh ginger, peeled and grated

1 teaspoon herbes de Provence

½ teaspoon salt

½ cup red wine vinegar

1 package (8 ounces) cream cheese

Fresh basil sprigs (optional)

Assorted crackers

Slow Cooker Directions

1. Place onion, tomatoes, sugar, garlic, ginger, herbes de Provence and salt in slow cooker. Pour in red wine vinegar; stir gently to mix. Cover; cook on LOW 4 to 5 hours or on HIGH 3 hours, stirring occasionally. Let mixture cool before using.

2. To serve, slice cream cheese in half horizontally (use unflavored dental floss for clean cut). Spread ⅓ cup tomato mixture onto one cream cheese half. Top with second cream cheese half and spread ⅓ cup tomato mixture on top. Garnish with fresh basil sprigs and serve with crackers. Refrigerate or freeze remaining tomato mixture for another use. *Makes 8 servings*

Note: The torte may be assembled in advance, wrapped and refrigerated until serving time.

Pressed Party Sandwich

1 (12-inch) unsliced loaf hearty peasant bread or sourdough bread

1½ cups fresh basil leaves

6 ounces thinly sliced smoked provolone or mozzarella cheese (about 9 slices)

3 plum tomatoes, sliced

1 red onion, thinly sliced*

2 roasted red bell peppers

2 to 3 tablespoons extra virgin olive oil

1 tablespoon balsamic vinegar

¼ teaspoon salt

¼ teaspoon black pepper

To reduce an onion's harshness when it will be eaten raw, place the slices in a sieve or colander and rinse under cold running water. Pat dry before use.

1. Cut bread in half lengthwise. Place halves cut side up on work surface. Gently pull out some of interior, leaving at least 1½-inch bread shell.

2. Layer basil, cheese, tomatoes, onion and roasted peppers on bottom half of loaf; drizzle with oil and vinegar. Sprinkle with salt and pepper; cover with top of loaf.

3. Wrap sandwich tightly in plastic wrap; place on baking sheet. Top with another baking sheet. Place canned goods or heavy pots and pans on top of baking sheet. Refrigerate sandwich several hours or overnight.

4. To serve, remove weights and plastic wrap from sandwich. Cut sandwich into 1-inch-thick slices; arrange on serving platter.

Makes 12 slices

Torta Rustica

1 tablespoon vegetable oil

1½ cups chopped onions

1 cup chopped carrots

2 cloves garlic, minced

1½ teaspoons salt, divided

2 medium zucchini, cubed

½ pound mushrooms, sliced

1 can (16 ounces) whole tomatoes, drained, chopped

1 can (15 ounces) artichoke hearts, drained, cut into halves

1 medium red bell pepper, seeded and cut into 1-inch pieces

1 teaspoon dried basil

½ teaspoon dried oregano

Salt and black pepper

1 package (about 15 ounces) refrigerated pie crusts

2 cups (8 ounces) shredded provolone or mozzarella cheese

1. Preheat oven to 400°F. Grease 2-quart casserole or soufflé dish.

2. Heat oil in large saucepan over medium heat. Add onions, carrots and garlic; cook and stir 5 minutes or until vegetables are tender. Stir in zucchini, mushrooms, tomatoes, artichoke hearts, bell pepper, basil and oregano. Season with salt and pepper. Bring to a boil over high heat. Reduce heat to low; cover and simmer 10 minutes.

3. Press one crust into casserole allowing dough to extend one inch over edge. Spoon half of vegetable mixture into casserole. Sprinkle with 1 cup of cheese; repeat layers.

4. Place remaining crust over filling. Fold edge of top crust over bottom and pinch to seal. Bake 30 to 35 minutes or until crust is golden brown, covering edge of dough with foil if necessary to prevent overbrowning. *Makes 6 servings*

Layered Mexican-Style Casserole

2 cans (about 15 ounces each) hominy, drained*

1 can (about 15 ounces) black beans, rinsed and drained

1 can (about 14 ounces) diced tomatoes with garlic, basil and oregano

1 cup thick and chunky salsa

1 can (6 ounces) tomato paste

½ teaspoon ground cumin

3 (9-inch) flour tortillas

2 cups (8 ounces) shredded Monterey Jack cheese

¼ cup sliced black olives

Hominy is corn that has been treated to remove the germ and hull. It can be found with the canned vegetables or beans in most supermarkets.

Slow Cooker Directions

1. Prepare foil handles (see below). Spray slow cooker with nonstick cooking spray.

2. Combine hominy, beans, tomatoes, salsa, tomato paste and cumin in large bowl.

3. Press 1 tortilla in bottom of slow cooker. (Edges of tortilla may turn up slightly.) Top with one third of hominy mixture and one third of cheese. Repeat layers. Top with remaining tortilla and hominy mixture; set aside remaining cheese.

4. Cover; cook on LOW 6 to 8 hours. Sprinkle with remaining cheese and olives. Cover; let stand 5 minutes. Pull out tortilla stack with foil handles.

Makes 6 servings

Foil Handles: Tear off three (18×2-inch) strips of heavy-duty foil or use regular foil folded to double thickness. Crisscross foil strips in spoke design and place into slow cooker to make lifting of tortilla stack easier.

Acknowledgments

The publisher would like to thank the companies and organizations listed below for the use of their recipes and photographs in this publication.

California Olive Industry

Campbell Soup Company

Dole Food Company, Inc.

Ortega®, A Division of B&G Foods, Inc.

Reckitt Benckiser Inc.

Sargento® Foods Inc.

Unilever

Wisconsin Milk Marketing Board

VOLUME MEASUREMENTS (dry)

1/8 teaspoon = 0.5 mL
1/4 teaspoon = 1 mL
1/2 teaspoon = 2 mL
3/4 teaspoon = 4 mL
1 teaspoon = 5 mL
1 tablespoon = 15 mL
2 tablespoons = 30 mL
1/4 cup = 60 mL
1/3 cup = 75 mL
1/2 cup = 125 mL
2/3 cup = 150 mL
3/4 cup = 175 mL
1 cup = 250 mL
2 cups = 1 pint = 500 mL
3 cups = 750 mL
4 cups = 1 quart = 1 L

VOLUME MEASUREMENTS (fluid)

1 fluid ounce (2 tablespoons) = 30 mL
4 fluid ounces (1/2 cup) = 125 mL
8 fluid ounces (1 cup) = 250 mL
12 fluid ounces (1 1/2 cups) = 375 mL
16 fluid ounces (2 cups) = 500 mL

WEIGHTS (mass)

1/2 ounce = 15 g
1 ounce = 30 g
3 ounces = 90 g
4 ounces = 120 g
8 ounces = 225 g
10 ounces = 285 g
12 ounces = 360 g
16 ounces = 1 pound = 450 g

DIMENSIONS

1/16 inch = 2 mm
1/8 inch = 3 mm
1/4 inch = 6 mm
1/2 inch = 1.5 cm
3/4 inch = 2 cm
1 inch = 2.5 cm

OVEN TEMPERATURES

250°F = 120°C
275°F = 140°C
300°F = 150°C
325°F = 160°C
350°F = 180°C
375°F = 190°C
400°F = 200°C
425°F = 220°C
450°F = 230°C

BAKING PAN SIZES

Utensil	Size in Inches/Quarts	Metric Volume	Size in Centimeters
Baking or Cake Pan (square or rectangular)	8×8×2	2 L	20×20×5
	9×9×2	2.5 L	23×23×5
	12×8×2	3 L	30×20×5
	13×9×2	3.5 L	33×23×5
Loaf Pan	8×4×3	1.5 L	20×10×7
	9×5×3	2 L	23×13×7
Round Layer Cake Pan	8×1½	1.2 L	20×4
	9×1½	1.5 L	23×4
Pie Plate	8×1¼	750 mL	20×3
	9×1¼	1 L	23×3
Baking Dish or Casserole	1 quart	1 L	—
	1½ quart	1.5 L	—
	2 quart	2 L	—